Gordon Baxter

Flying Lessons
and Pilot Talk

Table of Contents

INTRODUCTION

By Gordon Baxter (1977, from his book titled "Bax Seat")

As you go through this book you will hear a certain constancy in these stories. They are love stories, pure as the Elizabethan ballads sung by Mamma Maybelle and the Carter Sisters from deep in the valleys of the Great Smoky Mountains. First come the trials and sorrows, then satisfaction to a heart that is true. Stories of a life-long love affair with airplanes.

I was one of those lucky kids born in the Golden Age of Aviation. I caught the twilight of barnstorming. Paid a 1933 fortune of five dollars to ride with Clarence Chamberlin in a Curtiss Condor, a gigantic old fabric box kite. Filled out my log book with rides in an OX Robin, a Stinson tri-motor that belonged to Billy Rose. Travel Airs, Wacos, a Lincoln-Page, a spin in a Fleet.

Flying Magazine found me down on the Gulf Coast of Texas where for 25 years I had produced my own radio and TV shows. Sort of the morning mouth of Beaumont.

Flying Magazine is put together in Manhattan, but most of the writing has come from little fields, far west of the Hudson River. I commented on this once to Robert B. Parke, then my editor-in-chief. That urbane New Yorker's explanation was: "to avoid the Manhattan syndrome."

Were it not for that practice, I would never have begun my long, loose and mostly happy relationship with Flying Magazine.

One night, in a Third Avenue bar, my mentor

at Flying Magazine, Stephan Wilkinson, leaned across the table to me and cried out, "Baxter, for over eight years you have been writing the same story for me!"

"But Stephan," I explained, "you keep buying it."

I guess that, if anything, I am the romance writer for Flying Magazine. Once, after one of the few attempts to have me do a pilot report on a new product, Stephan sent the fourth rewrite attempt back to me with a sizzling "Baxter, the trouble with you is that you never met an airplane you didn't like!"

At a product breakfast at the Reading Air Show an avionics company president introduced his new line by starting out with "Now that we can dispel all the romance and view the airplane as a useful tool ..." That's all I stayed for. I not only did not like the way that Yankee pronounced it "useful twe-el," but I really have no reason to stay in the same room with a man who believes there is no more romance in flying. Even if he just bought me breakfast.

The ruination of my boyhood ambition to be an Army pursuit ship pilot and then to fly for the airlines had been accurately forecast by a high school math teacher: "If you don't pay attention and stop drawing airplanes, you will not be smart enough to even get in the gate at Randolph Field."

That's exactly how it turned out.

But the germination of my ambition to be a pilot never died. By 1957 I could afford to solo a headstrong Luscombe, which circled me three times on the ground and then mowed itself out of sight in a sorghum field, where my instructor, A.M. Vanneman, eventually located me and said, "Well. We ain't gone leave it out here, are we?"

I also nearly memorized and completely wore out my first copies of Ernest K. Gann's *Fate Is the*

Hunter and Saint Exupery's *Night Flight*. Those two were my graduate school, and I still go back to them when I feel a dryness of the soul.

I read Flying and Air Progress Magazines during the late '60s. Flying was read in a scholarly manner, Air Progress because it then still carried the vestiges of my beloved War Birds tales.

I wanted to write airplane stories, and they kept bubbling to the surface like tar in summer, but it would have never occurred to me to send any of the stuff to a real magazine. So I printed it in the Kountze News.

The Kountze News came out every Thursday in the little Eastex town of Kountze, with a press run of about 1,400 papers. The shaggy old editor, Archer Fullingim, paid me in mayhaw jelly and gourds.

There was not an aviator in the town.

One day in 1970, Archie Trammell, then Senior Editor for Flying Magazine, came to town to address the local Rotary Club. I snared Archie for an interview on the morning broadcast.

He was in a hurry, but I caught him in the door and pressed some of my Kountze News airplane stories into his hand. Archie scanned them, standing on one foot, then looked up at me and spoke the words that became my writing contract with Flying Magazine: "Why aren't you writing for us?"

PREFACE

My father, Gordon Baxter, passed away in 2005. To many of his fans, he was known as Bax. The column he wrote for Flying magazine was titled "Bax Seat."

He was passionate about flying and the people he met through aviation. His talent and friendships took him from grassy airports around Texas to fancy watering holes in New York City.

Whether on the radio or with a typewriter, Bax loved to tell stories. He loved the magic of flying and the power of history. With his quirky storytelling, Bax did more than entertain audiences and readers; he recorded the history of his place and time.

"I have lived when a trip of 50 miles meant the entire day, counting the wait for the river ferries and changing a tire on the old Dodge a time of two," he would tell audiences.

"One way an author can judge the worth of his writing is to look back on it after it gets old and see if there is any worth still in it." Who said that?

Gordon Baxter wrote that, as the introduction to his book *Bax Seat,* published in 1977.

That same piece of writing now serves as the introduction to this book, the first collection of Gordon Baxter's work to be published in the twenty-first century.

Jenny T. Baxter
December 2021

Chapter 1
The Two Faces of Pilots

In flying there is the "official face," as in textbooks, talking to the press, or to any outsiders, and there is the "other face," the way pilots really talk to each other. The two never mix.

"There are old pilots, and there are bold pilots," we will honestly tell you, "but there are no old bold pilots." We all know this, and we believe it.

You will find out, soon after you are among us at the airport, that when any two or more of us gather we relish telling hair-raising tales of how bold we are; of the dangerous flying we have done, the rules we have bent, and the junky old airplanes we have survived. The stories are great, and they all have the same ending—about how once again we have cheated fate.

From the very beginning, better heads than mine have puzzled over aviation's wonderful schizophrenia; wondered why pilots, already engaged in the unforgiving act of flying, will deliberately take chances and seem to enjoy it—and enjoy the telling of it.

Hearing about the wild stuff that pilots do, and the awful wrecks it gets them into, is highly entertaining. One of the most serious and responsible aviation magazines knows this and eases their guilt by running such stories as true confessions, or as little morality plays, with all the exciting details still intact, but with a lesson for you at the end. Reader surveys show that it is one of the most popular features of the magazine. It is the only instance I can think of when you will come close to hearing the two faces of aviation speaking from one mouth.

Every strata of aviation is touched by our tendency to have fun with something as serious as flying airplanes. Airline pilots are the best trained among us. They are the most conservative of men. They set the standards for millions of hours flown safely. You have really got to be in the family to sit in on such stories as the one about the ferry crew who slow-rolled an empty DC-9. Or of the flat-out, down (on the deck) racing between two competitive airlines that flew the same kinds of planes over the same short route. Or agreeing on the cover-up story after landing at the wrong airport. "We had a fire warning light, and this was only a precautionary landing."

Legendary among line pilots' bar stories is the one about the old captain found napping as his transport plane flew on autopilot above solid cloud cover toward a coastline city. His crew reset all of his navigation instruments to read "from" the target city instead of "to." Then they, too, pretended to be asleep and set off the low-fuel warning signal. All this to give the old skipper a few fine moments of awakening to alarms and wondering when he had flown over his destination and how far out over the ocean he was now. They let him sweat a moment before straightening him out. Sure, the ole man was mad, but what could he say?

Former airline captain Ernie Gann has flown thousands of safe, scheduled, and uneventful hours, yet his best-selling masterpiece, *Fate is the Hunter,* is a retelling of those brief moments in his life when everything went wrong, when courage and skill rode supreme, and the pilots involved barely escaped with their skins. His dialogue between two pilots meeting on the other side of that "employees only" door is classic:

"Where have you been?"

"Lost, what did you expect?"

"Your personal effects."

Had you met Captain Gann as a passenger you would have met a slight, modest, and highly professional aviator. But ole Gann collected all the great hangar tales, and we loved them. You will notice, however, that he drew the shades down and never fully identified the pilots or the airlines. He couldn't. Because Ernie had let you come into the back of the hangar and listen to the forbidden tales.

As you begin to hear hangar tales, you will quickly note that the macho image of the silk-scarf hero pilot is a factor both in the stories and in the accidents.

There is plenty of sex in airplanes. In their free movement through liquid air, in the sensory response of flying them, in the very phallic shape of some of them. You don't have to be a dirty old Freudian reject to look at the long, rounded lines of the Corsair, the Navy's famed World War II fighter plane, and imagine yourself loose in the combat skies over Bali with all that potency and power–fingering life or death with a thumb rubbed against the little red gun button on the joystick. Thirty years after the war, "Pappy" Boynton's story *Baa Baa Black Sheep* still sold, and the TV series of those Corsairs, peeling off into the death dives, competed well for a long time against *Charlie's Angels*.

><

There is plenty of sex in airplanes, but no sexism is intended in this book when I repeatedly call the instructor "him" or the student "he." Women learn to fly as easily as men, sometimes better,

3

because so much of flying is gentle coordination and being able to maintain a prolonged attention span over small details. The chances are good and so is your luck if you find a woman flight instructor. You seldom hear the common complaints of rudeness and impatience from their students.

Women were not particularly welcomed into flying by men, who preferred to keep the mystique to themselves. The first women pilots who persisted in pushing themselves into this male world were regarded even by their own home-and-hearth sisters as being tinged by the same faintly racy reputation that is associated with stage actresses. For what it's worth, all of those early dare-devil women pilots were beautiful.

In later years, a sisterhood of women pilots was formed around the memory of Amelia Earhart, best known of women aviators. The group, called the Ninety-Nines, is a sort of shelter and supportive organization of housewives, mothers, and businesswomen who persist in flying. As a guest speaker at one of the Ninety-Nines' conventions, I stood up and told them that getting used to seeing women in command of airliners and military planes was going to take me a little time. But I had no objection to the idea, and some of my best friends are women pilots, said I. They took me out onto the patio and threw me into the pool.

I must admit that the sexual overtones of flying were a part of the image that attracted me to it. I pictured myself, helmet and goggles, white scarf and big wristwatch, leaning against the fireplace. Crooked smile, but even teeth. The only trouble with this was that by the time I got around to being a pilot, wearing wings had gone out of style. I still have the old leather jacket and the big wristwatch, but there were so many of us pilots lined up against the fireplace that nobody noticed anymore. You'll have to ask your instructor to explain about the legend of the pilot's big wristwatch.

Only in South and Central America can one still find vestiges of the great traditional male sexist-pig pilot. A few years ago, I rode a DC-3 out of Bogota, Colombia. The pilot was dapper, with a handsome cookie-dust mustache riding his upper lip. He flew low over the jungle, dodging thunderstorms, somehow locating each little jungle-clearing airstrip with its row of shacks beside the dirt runway. At each clearing, as the dust of his prop wash settled over the storefronts and excited passengers crowded out to meet the plane, a beautiful maiden of the village would come out to him. They would stand and talk softly in the shade of the wing on the offside from all the freight and passenger loading. They talked earnestly, while he nibbled the ice cream bar she had brought to him. At departure time she would cling to him, pressing her tip-toed body to him in farewell. He seemed to be reassuring her of his faithful and early return. Then he would stroll over a little way, turn his back to her and the passengers watching from the windows, and with care and ceremony, standing there in his blue uniformed coat, he would urinate upon a post. He did this at each of the jungle villages on his schedule. Truly one of the last of a great tradition of airline pilots. Nowadays all you can see them doing in the small terminals of America is eating the ice cream.

There is plenty of sex in airplanes, and in the beginning of airline travel, as now, pretty young women were used as bait. But my wife, a former Braniff hostess, tells me that the real reason for the beautiful stewardesses in the early days when air travel was considered very daring was to "have us stand by that coffin-shaped cabin entry as if to say to all those guys standing there with their knees knocking, 'See, even a little girl can do it.'"

And the legends of the stewardess logging "laptime" with the pilot are true. Although my wife says she sat in the pilot's seat alone instead of in the pilot's lap, she admits that there was nothing so lovely as piloting a huge airliner, boring steadily and smoothly into the velvet night over the Rockies, while those trusting souls slept fitfully back in the cabin, not dreaming that the stewardess might be flying the plane.

An old friend who flies for Eastern tells of one starry night when his co-pilot and the stewardess were logging a little laptime. "I saw a reflection pass over the instruments and realized that the cabin door had silently swung open and all the passengers could see her dangling legs and her curled-up toes. I asked her if she meant to leave the door open and she said she could never go back in the cabin and face all those people ever again.

My wife took her own days as aircrew seriously, but enjoys the stories, as we all do. She resents the sex-kitten image of her former profession. As for her own prudence, she pointed out that any crew base is as gossipy as a small-town party line, and a girl makes and lives with her reputation. But what griped her was this: "All you businessmen looking us up and down as we stand there in the aisle and demonstrate the use of the emergency equipment and tell how to evacuate the cabin. Records of actual crash landings show that those same heroes will sit panic-stricken in their seats in a burning cabin while us 'chicks' direct the evacuation. But that is what we are trained for, and that's one of the real reasons for cabin crews."

Another of the persistent smirks of sex and airplanes is the Mile-High Club. Remaining overnight with a companion in a Denver hotel will not qualify you. Nor, according to Tony Page, will any experience with your mate in any aircraft equipped with an autopilot. Tony is a good example of sex and sexism in aviation. She is a veteran pilot, rated in both airplanes and helicopters, but when she began publishing her little tabloid aviation newspaper, *X-Country News,* Tony changed her name to the masculine spelling Tony for fear that an aviation paper published by a woman would lack credibility in the male world she was a part of.

Sex and airplanes is not all Freudian fantasy, dirty jokes, and subliminal associations with the sensually free movement of planes through the air-ocean. It is also a part of the real-world tendency of the human animal to have some fun.

I have a friend who flies a Stearman biplane high over the sunny hills of California with his lady sunbathing in the rear cockpit. And I will admit to a few occasions of nude Mooney flying. On a long solo flight my cabin gets cramped and stuffy, and I get bored and clothesbound. So, I fly my little plane sans suit. It's as much fun as a skinny-dip in a secluded fresh country creek, up there in the high, cool, clear sunlight. I can't find anything in the Federal Air Regulations that says this is illegal.

Yet, until now, I have been careful about whom I admitted this to. More of the two faces of flying–the stern, moralistic code of behavior that draws a sharp line between the way pilots really do talk and act, and the way we all agree we should talk and act.

All of us, in our official face, deplore the white flying scarf of the hangar tales. The most careful pilot I know is editor of one of the "official" magazines, and he does not write about, or practice, any fooling around in airplanes. Yet he relishes the challenge of flying expertly in really gunky weather. Give him a low icy day that I wouldn't even get out of bed for and he flies – his white scarf secretly streaming.

><

You can find the two faces of flying among the astronauts, the most tight-lipped, ice-water-for-blood pilots that America has ever produced. In the heyday of our space exploration program, the national reporters complained out loud that they couldn't get anything out of these guys but official Eagle Scout talk. They still can't today. Only in Walt Cunningham's book, the *All-American Boys,* did Walt, an astronaut himself, come clean about all the fun you may have suspected that they were having.

In order to maintain their razor edge of skill at flying high-performance aircraft, the astronauts were given access to the T-38 Talon, a supersonic jet fighter-trainer. Cunningham described it as an unbelievably beautiful airplane and said few women could resist an invitation to come ride in one.

Cunningham pointed out that with its faster than sound speed, an astronaut could finish up his morning space training at Houston, spend the afternoon visiting with friends out on the West Coast, and be back home in Houston that night. He tells how they played with the airplane. Going out to the coast against the prevailing westerly winds, they had to make a fuel stop at El Paso. Returning to Texas, there was a chance that they could catch strong, favorable tail winds and make it home without stopping. They would crap shoot with the high westward jet stream air currents just for the fun of trying to make it back to Houston non-stop; for the blood-tingling experience of letting it all hang out, as Walt phrased it; for the kick of getting fuel-exhaustion flame-out as they turned off the ramp at Houston.

Why this brinkmanship? This streak of madness?

"To put your life in danger from time to time breeds a saneness in dealing with trivialities." That was not uttered by some ace rocket pilot. That was written by Nevil Shute, born 1900, educated at Oxford in science, a distinguished British aircraft designer and noted novelist.

Tom Wolfe also attempted to come to grips with this flyer's combination of courage and foolishness. He borrowed the astronaut's own phrase for it as the title of his book, *The Right Stuff*.

This macho stuff is not always so right. The Navy long ago recognized the trait as part of what makes a good fighter pilot, but also recognized that such men were high on the accident-prone list. The Navy has tried to channel the daredevil urges with a contempt campaign. They call dangerous, show-off style flying "flat-hatting," and such pilots are known as "Dilberts." The Navy will also take back your golden wings and the little blue box they came in if it can hang reckless flying on you.

Ag pilots are another group of professionals trying to clean up their act, and they must fly low and slow for a living. Their first move was to quit calling themselves "duster pilots," and all of their meetings and publications became unbelievably official and stuffy. Yet the ad men, who are still in touch with what duster pilots are really like, run ads in their own official magazine showing a giant, 1,200-horsepower biplane and call it the Diablo. They show the pilot as a raunchy-looking ace standing spread-legged by the wingtip, helmet, sunglasses, and all, and the copy reads, "Can you handle this devil's challenge?"

The two faces of aviation. We is and we ain't.

><

Airline pilots not only never talk about their pranks in public, but there is a mysterious cutoff point where they also pretend that none of it ever happens when dealing with each other. In any official business, such as a check ride with each other, they are formal, demanding, and often call each other "Mr." or "Sir."

There is poorly concealed contempt for any pilot who persists in Dilbert-style flying. There seems to be a tolerance for a few blunders now and then, but if this turns out to be your pattern of flying, your hangar stories will start to be shunned. Here, in descending order, are the basic top ten hangar tales and the degree of their social acceptance.

1. Wild landings and takeoffs
2. Dealing heroically with in-flight mechanical failures
3. Getting lost and finding your way home
4. Getting lost and not finding your way home
5. Buzzing your loved one's house
6. Running out of gas
7. A crash you can walk away from
8. Flying into bad weather
9. Flying while drinking or doping
10. Getting killed in a crash

You will notice that all classic hangar tales deal with survival. If you have the misfortune to be killed in an airplane, your story will go around just once. Then you, and the event that carried you away, will never be mentioned again.

Hangar flying can be instructional. We learn from the other guy's misfortunes. We have often joked that the time spent listening to these tales should be allowed in the student pilot's logbook. Maybe at only 50 percent value, since at least half of it is lies.

But the other-face-of-flying stories can be much more gripping to hear and easier to remember than the lessons from the pedantic teachings of the official face. Here is an example:

Once there was a hotshot Stearman pilot who rented one of those grand old biplanes and went off to buzz his girlfriend's house. She lived on a mountainside in North Carolina in a cottage shaded by tall trees. Hearing the mighty roar of her hero's engine, she trotted out and waved prettily from the yard. Swooping by his lady love, doing a low slow turn and waving back to her, the pilot hung his Stearman in one of the tall trees beside her house. The mighty hardwood uprooted with the snared Stearman in its branches. The impact of the airplane uprooted the tree and it all went rolling, shouting, and crashing down the mountainside, making a terrible mess. The wonderful old Stearman was balled up forever, the grand old shade tree was gone, the pilot's girlfriend quit him, and the FBO who had rented the airplane ran him off for good. And this true story is still being told in the mountain country south of Ashville.

Now isn't that more memorable and picturesque than me just trying to tell you that low and slow turns are more dangerous than they appear to be?

As we said in the beginning, unless you are already suffering in the comradeship of aviators, do not expect to just drop in at the airport and begin to enjoy the benefits of hangar flying. The chatter among pilots will dry up as soon as a stranger approaches. They may look at you with the innocent eyes of teenagers found in a room full of smoke when nobody appears to be smoking anything.

It is not uncommon to remain on somewhat reserved terms with your instructor during the interim of student flying or have a dual relationship with his official face in the airplane, and the other face on the ground.

So when, you might rightfully ask, do you get past your new boy at the club status and become a part of the other face of flying? It will begin the day something happens to you. The day you burst into the pilot's coffee room full of excitement and cry out, "Did you guys see that last landing? That thing must have bounced hangar high. I bet I left permanent dents in that runway!" And they will all laugh and agree that you are probably the most inept student that anyone here can remember.

But this will not be the story you will take home with you that day to tell your folks, who warned you not to take up flying. They would not understand the language or the circumstances, and anyway, you want them to think well of aviation. We are still selling the general public on the idea that flying is a good thing.

So you will suppress all that which is going on inside you. They will ask, "How did flying go today?"

And you will grin at the memory of how it really went today, and tell them, "Just fine. We're in the landing syllabus now."

The two faces of flying.

Chapter 2
Me and My Rating

Instrument flying, I had concluded, is an unnatural act, probably punishable by God. Even if it isn't, the whole idea of flying an airplane when you can't see out the window seems self-defeating.

I knew a few instrument pilots. Technicians. The type who would read the marriage manual on their wedding night, or sip Coca-Cola at a party when everyone else was being thrown into the pool. I have a friend—a doctor, a little steel-rimmed guy with bald pate and the strongest, coldest fingers, like forceps. He flies his Mooney just exactly like in the book. His approaches leave a crisp dotted line in the clouds. He bugs me.

I respected instrument pilots, understand. Awed by them and their sudden popping out of the lead belly of a cloud and taxiing up to where we stood, huddled like fluffed-up birds under the dripping eaves. Getting out with their little secret chart books. Who is this Jeppesen, anyway? I peeked at those flimsy little chicken-track charts. No rivers, no railroads, no drive-in theaters, all written in Egyptian. No rosy colors to tingle a pilot's imagination.

I put aside any idea of my ever flying instruments. I'm going to be a low-time pilot all my life. Flying since 1957, yet the total hours stay below the magic thousand. A very sparse ticket, lots of white space around those words, "private–SEL." That's for SEL-dom. I had heard that instrument flying was such a demanding skill that unless a pilot went out and flew in the clouds often enough, his rating would turn to ashes in his wallet. Why should I be an instrument pilot? Would you trust a part-time brain surgeon?

Anyway, being a VFR pilot kept things exciting. Residents of small Texas towns still wonder about that madman circling their water tanks in rainstorms. Or the guy who flew a Champ down Main Street to read the name on the post office. (Had to. All it said on the school bus was School Bus.) Come to think of it, the IH (interstate highway) approach system has never been openly credited. Think of its merits: You are too low to be hit by other airplanes, too high for the cars; no TV towers grow in the middle of the interstate; and if you stay with it, it's bound to take you somewhere.

Flying VFR all these thrilling years has kept me in touch with America's heartland. The farmer on his tractor, shaking his fist. The big, shiny roaches in the No-Tell Motel during unexpected little overnight stays. The thrill of eventually finding my way home again and that phone call to my widow—I mean wife—"Cheated death again!"

I admit it: I was nervous about some things. Like being around the Feds, for instance; and omni navigation. Remember now, those gadgets crept into airplanes long after I started flying. (I always meant to ask why one day you fly toward the needle, other days away from it.) But with a good pipeline right-of-way underneath me, I could usually get it sorted out after a while.

I really hated going into big, busy airports. All those chaps snapping at each other in strange languages; and something about approach frequencies, which I decided not to fool with. I'd just fly up low, real close to the tower and say, friendly like, "Hi, this is ol' Cessna Two-Niner Betsy, can I land with y'all?" I don't know why that seemed to get everybody's noses out of joint.

Well, as you have no doubt noticed, instrument pilots are evangelistic. "Bax, you really ought to get your ticket."

"Yeah, sure. I already got one." And I'd whip out my blue card with the hole in it and hold it up against the sky and read what it says on it: "When color of card matches color of sky, fly." I believed in that. Like Pappy Sheffield always said to his students out at our little grass airport, "Keep one wing in the sunshine and keep smiling."

That's true, too. You look at the face of a pilot who has both wings in the cloud. He looks positively gloomy.

Finally, one of those evangelists got to me. Jerry Griffin; runs a Piper outfit over at the cement airport. Calls it Professional Aviation. They wear coats and ties, shave every day, and keep those little stubby airplanes waxed so slick that a fly landing on one would break a leg. I respect and admire Jerry. He's the blue-eyed, blonde-haired, all-American kid who grew up at the airport fence. His operation is his dream come true.

Jerry is a "non-stress" instructor, as Bob Blodget used to say. After I got used to the funny way the Pipers ran down the cement and popped into the air, I began to look forward to the hours under the hood beside him. He purred, blending with the purr of the low-winger. I remember the enchantment of those first hours with Jerry. He gave me the confidence that I could defy all the senses that all my ancestors had developed since they came down out of the trees and began to walk on their hind legs. I was fascinated with the little science-fiction world that grew in the green-and-white glow of the needles and numbers. I had my own horizon, my own gravity. We flew into the sunset, into the nights, into the clouds. It made no difference, for I had my own little universe swimming before my eyes.

Gradually, the instruments came to translate into attitudes of flight; they became an intellectualized extension of my own senses. Drunk with professionalism, I went right out and bought a black attaché case and some bifocals. It was the first time I had ever needed a place to keep papers while flying or needed to know what all those little close-together marks on the dials meant.

Somewhere along in here, Jerry sent my license off to Oklahoma City and it came back with a blue seal upon it. Now, at least, I would not be an automatic dead man in 120 seconds if I flew into a cloud.

Griffin said the instrument flight test would come easy enough, in time, but we were both worried about that glass mountain ahead: the written exam. In real life, I am the morning mouth on local radio. On a disc jockey's schedule, that meant early to bed, early to rise, attend a night school and look more dead than alive. So Jerry did a noble thing; he referred me to the Bob Marsh Aviation School, on Houston Hobby Field. After that, I'd pass the written in a matter of days, I was assured.

My first thought was that Marsh operated a diploma mill. His school teaches the FAA exams, and I never heard of anybody failing to pass a written when Bob Marsh sent them reeling off to the Fed's exam room nearby. I went to Marsh expecting three days of cram, wham, bam, thank you ma'am, but I was staggered by the mass of knowledge needed and the relentless digging into a massive pile of Government publications to get to it.

Marsh gives the student a dummy exam, the student researches his answers, wrong ones are circled on the graded paper and the student has to display a complete working knowledge of every subject missed during a mano a mano oral review with an instructor. The process simply goes on and on until the student has learned this new vocabulary and all its attendant rules and can snap out the correct answer to every squiggly blur on a weather-depiction map and every bird footprint on a Jepp chart.

Marsh says he builds his study course around the FAA written-exam format so that the student will be familiar with it when he sees the real thing. He has mastered a workable technique of imprinting "Government-speak" upon the clay of a student's mind.

After three days of this, all I wanted was out. I kept gazing off toward distant blue skies, longing to find a place not boxed in, so I could lay the Stearman over on its back and shout "Ya-a-a-ah!" I was never born to fly with a bunch of books in my lap.

Marsh, who learned to fly from Moses, and had retired as chief pilot for Howard Hughes, shook his fine silver head and looked wonderfully sad. "There's only one learning obstacle I cannot overcome in a student—lack of motivation." We parted with regrets, but as friends.

> <

A few years rolled by. Flying published its Guide for Instrument Flying 1973. The demand exceeded the supply, and the magazine soon became a collector's item.

Plans were made for a sequel. The New York office searched its roster of far-flung editor-writers. "Who is our most hard-case VFR pilot?"

"How about Bax? He doesn't even like to sit indoors in a cabin ... He's nearly 50, a part-time flyer, set in his ways ... If he can get a ticket, anybody can."

"We can really make a case for instrument flying ..." And so the Word went forth.

I kicked. I screamed. Bled real blood. Offered to fly around the world in a Champ with one hand tied behind my back. Said I'd grow a moustache and write about a talking seagull. Anything but this. Didn't they realize it would be the ruination of one of America's last unspoiled pasture pilots? Anyway, I never got a chance to read Guide for Instrument Flying. They never got as far as the grass airport in Texas.

New York sent a copy. I read it, and it like to have scared me to death. All this nonchalant tossing off of such phrases as: "Of course, anyone can keep the airplane right side up." Hell, I couldn't.

But if this cup cannot be passed, then let us drink the most bitter portion first. In November of 1972, I once more appeared before Bob Marsh, hat in hand, asking for a go at the written exam. His only comment was a bear hug, and that he had been expecting me.

We mounted an all-out campaign, and this I recommend to any busy man. Get your affairs in order; take about a week off; and present yourself to a reputable, well-organized ground school and concentrate on dat ol' debbil, the written exam. The flying part of it will make more sense to you later.

In order for me to live with this ground-school monster for a week, a most strange business alliance was worked out, involving the publishers of Flying, the owners of Radio KLVI and a 19-year-old Houston bride. We moved the radio station from Beaumont, Texas to Houston and installed it in the front bedroom of my newly wedded daughter's home, which is just blocks from Marsh's school on Hobby Field.

><

The housewives listening to my morning show got music, news and witty recitations of FAR Part 91. I was totally saturated with this new world of words; I couldn't shut it off. I went to sleep at night dreaming that I had my hands around the throat of whichever Government lawyer had written all that stuff. It couldn't have been written by a human pilot. It obviously was never intended to support an airplane in flight, only its own bulk in court.

I who had known the freedom of the hawk became a studying automaton. A sponge of the assorted knowledge that a man must arm himself with to fly without outside eyes ... true course is magnetic course, plus or minus variation ... magnetic heading plus or minus deviation equals compass heading ... the following documents must be displayed inside the aircraft ... Zulu minus six equals Central ... pressure altitude ... density altitude ... indicated airspeed ... calibrated airspeed ... true airspeed ... the hemoglobin absorbs carbon monoxide 200 times faster than oxygen ... My mind staggered. It reeled. It separated and rolled up into little balls. I had slit open the belly of the body of aviation and was swishing around in the innards, and I began to wish I'd never seen them. If it was going to take all of this just to fly by instruments, then ATRs must be gods. They should be allowed to ascend the flight deck adorned in silken garments, with private pilots as acolytes bearing candles.

For me, there was no way. I felt like a savage brought out of the jungle to be taught the whole body of civilization in one week. By the third day, I was silly, numb. My head felt as though it had been injected through the ear with numbered putty. Bob unchained me and sent me home. "Look at your handwriting. It's gone all to pieces. Go home, fix a drink, go to bed. Tomorrow will be worse."

On the last day before the exam, they heaped me with books. AIM, FAR, ZAP—all the stuff I needed to know, and all of it scattered through a million sub-paragraphs. If a lawyer had to go through this many slithering books and back-flopping pages to research a case, nothing would ever get to the courtroom. They would settle it out on the lawn with short-barreled pistols. Why doesn't somebody codify all this junk? I rebelled. I told Bob the hell with all this, teach me with words. Let me sit at your feet, tell it to me in real words as the ancient masters did. No man can read an FAR.

But inside me, the growling glow had begun. I was ready, and I knew it. I was stiff with it. For a week now, I felt as though I had been shackled with chains inside a wooden box only four feet high and four feet wide, new Government documents and a pan of water being shoved in through the trap door. After seven days and seven nights, I was ready. I sprang out into the daylight, all covered with hair, howling and gnashing to get to that real exam.

That FAA exam room was rectangular, white-walled, sterile, windowless except for the one-way-mirrored door. The matron, in a seersucker uniform with black name tag, ran her Geiger counter over my lunch bag. (Man, it's a six-hour exam.) The Geiger counter found my little transistorized calculator and shrilled its alarm.

Feds in dark coats with narrow ties came running softly. I explained that ever since the fourth grade, I had flunked anything to do with math, and what a shame to blow questions on weight and balance and time and distance just because the towers of figures toppled for me. A hurried conference over the exam rules found nothing that said such a device could not be used, "So long as it does not have a memory circuit," they warned. It didn't, and that little handful of transistors saved me about an hour and at least a half dozen wrong answers.

I entered into the stark chamber, my footballs crashing among the earlier inmates, who looked up, glaring, until I had rattled around and built my nest. From that time, the only sound was an occasional deep sigh—more like a drawn-out sob. Once some guy's stomach rumbled and I almost bolted and fled; thought the building was caving in.

Marsh had commanded, "Use those Mickey Mouse things I showed you. Place a strip of paper over the question and read it line for line. Move your lips if you have to. I've watched you read. You gulp a whole paragraph. Do that in there and you'll swallow the hook that's buried in the question for smart guys."

I drew up two columns on a scratch pad, headed "possible" and "out." Bob had said that every question would have four answers. "Two will be dogs, one will be the deceiver, one is the correct answer. Put the dog numbers in the 'out' column. Then you just have two answers to consider. Then think, man, because if you don't have a full knowledge of the intent of the question, the deceiver will appear to be the most believable answer."

A part of Bob's Last Rites and Benediction ceremony is to challenge the applicant to predict his score and write it down in secret. Bob does the same, and a two-bit bet is made on the outcome. I gave myself a four-point spread; 68 to 72. Bob had written down 78. When that ominous letter arrived from

Oklahoma City, my final score was exactly what that crafty, mean old man had predicted. He insisted on payment by check.

Rejoicing, I started for the door, free at last to go fly the airplane, the easy part. But another manacle had been slipped over my cuff. This time, the chain led to what you had better not call a Link Trainer, for it is in truth a Cessna 172 Flight Simulator—a one-of-a-kind modification of the Link. It will do anything a 172 will do, and some of it much more suddenly.

Had I but known what the next 19.2 hours in the green box would bring, I would have given up on the rating and put in for pit crew at Car and Driver.

"The airplane," said Professor Marsh, "is a very poor classroom. And if you cannot do the required stuff in the simulator, then you will have plenty of problems out there." So I climbed in and they shut the coffin lid.

If I said "Ahhhh" or "This is ..." then I had to start over. Me, with 28 years on broadcast radio—I began to get mike fright. They badgered me, and how I longed to get one of those instructors into my control room for just a day and make an ass out of him. But soon I was using this new-found skill with the radio as I commuted into Hobby by Cessna each day. Some hillbilly, like I used to be last week, would call up with 17 planes of the frequency and say, "Hobby Tower, Hobby Tower, this is Cessna November 1234 Alfa, and ahhh, we are ... about ... over downtown, ah, and we plan to land at Hobby, ah, what's y'all's active runway? Over."

Gritting my teeth like the rest during this soliloquy, I would wait for a breath of silence in the chatter and hit them with my carefully rehearsed "Hobby, Cessna 8529 Bravo, Fry Intersection with

Juliet." And like magic came, "Two-Niner Bravo, report right base 30." And just like that. In seven seconds, each of us knew all we needed to know about the other. I felt pretty smug, although it had taken me a week to find Fry Intersection.

But the confines of that little green box were paced off by Satan himself, and his footprints are called holding patterns. Paul Carrington taught me how to find my way into those little private cells of airspace. Direct entry, parallel entry or teardrop; what a delicious name for it: teardrop. Also sweat-drop. It got so bad that each day, I used a different brand of anti-perspirant. And each day, I surfaced from the box dripping like a fish. The laundry began to reject my shirts.

Big Brother's metallic voice became inescapable: "You are flying through your fix ... you are 100 feet above assigned altitude ... what is the reciprocal of 134? C'mon, c'mon!" And more nagging about radio technique: "Six-One Xray, say altitude."

"Twenty-two hundred."

"Never heard of it."

"Two thousand two hundred."

"That's better."

Time stopped in the green box. No yesterday, no tomorrow, just those walls closing in. Bunched up, I tried to cheat. I muttered, cursed, got vertigo, spun, crashed and burned on the VOR approach to Galveston. Once, I even stalled and crashed on takeoff. When that thing shuddered and broke and those needles started unwinding, I felt a shock of real fear in my chest. Slammed in power, dived for airspeed, actually died when the altimeter hit field elevation. Only the raucous laughter and beating on the box from outside, and the fact that my smoking hole was not 400 feet below sea level, brought my senses back.

Still, no one will ever make me believe that thing is just bolted to the floor.

I, an airplane pilot, was suffering the indignity of having to jiggle this internal bungee-cord-and-bellows box into level flight and keep it there among slithering needles. My red tracings on the plastic overlay outside looked like the homeward route of a drunk boll weevil. I alibied that the mechanical phoniness of the thing was impossible—that I could fly a real airplane. Then the immaculate Tony Koenninger stepped up on the running board, reached in with one hand and flew a perfect approach. For that, I could hate him. "The trouble with you, Bax, is that you have never flown a real airplane like we are asking you to here. Going home tonight in that 172, see if you can fly within five degrees of heading and 20 feet of altitude."

><

That was the beginning of the next great turnaround in my thinking about flying. I discovered what a sloppy pilot I had always been. I had been wandering along like a strutted cow coming in at milking time. I began to really try to nail those numbers. Soon it got to be a habit, and a second bud of pride—of wanting to be professional in flying—broke through the thick bark.

But it was still slow going in the box. I regressed for a time, and they put me back to basics. Depression led to savagery. I slammed it around, rejoicing as the bellows hissed and groaned. New clearances to copy piled upon corrections not yet made. In my great fury, I would have leaped out of that thing and punched my instructor, except that the years Tom Adams had spent in that flying trapeze called a helicopter had developed his biceps powerfully. Always, his voice would come in: "You can fight it, but you can never win. Make it come to you."

The urge to kill born in the simulator was not just mine. Tommy Reedy, a high-time ag pilot and part owner of Reedy-West Air Service, in Angleton, Texas, was going through the same torture an hour ahead of me. Tommy was in the school because "It's getting so you can't go anywhere VFR anymore." The quiet, taciturn Reedy once sprang from the infernal box and made Marsh a cash offer for the thing so he could take it home and chop it up with an ax.

Lorene Holmes, who was going the IFR route so she could be as good as her Beechcraft, could sometimes be heard softly weeping inside the infernal device. She suggested that a drain plug be installed in the cockpit floor so that a finished student could be poured out into a pan and set in the window to cool.

An hour of two in the box would dissolve me into utter stupidity. Once when turning right again instead of left for a teardrop entry, a ghostly voice whispered through the fuselage, "Left. Turn left." I later learned that there is a hidden peephole in the thing, so they can see how white your knuckles are, but I never found out who my prompting angel of mercy was.

Later, in the real airplane, I was being eaten up alive on a back-course approach into Hobby. I had forgotten about reverse sensing. Approach radar couldn't even tell whether I was heading for Hobby, Andrau or Ellington. A shaking cup of coffee in my hand, I told my instructor at debriefing that I didn't see how I had botched it up so badly; all the other times had been right down the slot. He gently reminded me that this had been my first one; all the "other times" had been in the simulator. That's how real the experience had seemed to me.

><

The campaign to get the instrument ticket had begun in early November. It was now approaching New Year's and the winter gunk had moved in over the Gulf Coast. I soon learned that if Hobby and Beaumont, my home base, were reporting VFR minimums, the clouds would be hugging the ground between the two, over the spooky Trinity River bottomlands over which I crept and cheated along Interstate 10. During this time, a Cherokee Six pilot trying the same stuff at Baytown got vertigo and slow-rolled in at the threshold of Humphrey Field, dispatching himself and his passengers.

There was only one tall obstruction along this course—the 570-foot-tall obelisk of the San Jacinto Battlefield Monument. My game was to find the white stone shaft in the haze and mist without hitting it. In wilder moments, I thought of what a fine way to go this would be:

"Say, whatever happened to your old man—the one who used to fly and write about it?"

"Oh, he hit the San Jacinto Monument in the fog one day. You can still see the mark, about halfway up to the star."

Tour guides would add this event to their spiel. A niche in Texas history. Oh, how I longed for that instrument rating, and how I hoped to live long enough to get it.

And now it was 1973, early January, and we were walking out to the real airplane for the first time. Bob Marsh's instrument trainer is a Cessna 172 bristling with antennas for almost every navaid except radar and inertial. It sat crushed low on its spats with its burden of electronics and long-range fuel tanks.

Each day began with one of those pre-flights that everyone ought to do but nobody does unless under the eye of the Feds or a flight instructor. As I inspected those little cotter keys that hold the aileron pins in place, as I have done on every Cessna for the last 15 years, I got to wondering where this custom started. Has there ever been a report of the ailerons falling off a Cessna? Does Dwane Wallace ever worry about those little bent wires? Later, in the course of 31.5 hours in that thing with Jim Shelton threatening to tape my hands if I didn't stop wigwagging those ailerons and zooming my turns all over the sky, I began to consider that while the cotter keys may never drop out, it did seem likely that I might wear them out.

Shelton and I droned through January together in the growing understanding and friendship that develops between men who fly side by side for long hours. The flight syllabus was a repetition of the pattern learned in the simulator. Radar vectors to a holding pattern, then to Galveston VOR, another hold, then the Galveston VOR approach, missed approach and back to Hobby for whatever instrument landing was in use. About two hours under the hood, with the worst saved for last, as it would be for real.

With the elastic headband of the hood slowly squeezing off the blood supply to my brain, I entertained Mr. Shelton with such comedy as attempting 180-degree intercepts to a radial and getting lost over the Galveston VOR. I was mildly surprised to learn that actual flight was even more demanding than those dark hours in the womb of the simulator. I say mildly, for by this time, I didn't really expect anything to be easy or turn out right. Shelton helped: He turned all the radios up to full blare to get me used to this new element of chaos. During the first few hours, he worked all communications; I had my hands full just keeping us right side up.

"Scan, man, don't stare at any one instrument ... take little bites at that radial intercept, then center those needles with the rudders ... hold that heading; in this business, flying a heading is everything ... pay attention ... concentrate ... this is an exercise in self-discipline ... quit flopping those ailerons; you want a five-degree correction, so skid into it."

And more: "I let you get lost over that VOR. Everybody does it sooner or later. You must keep a mental image of where you are relative to what those needles are telling you. If you ever lose the mental picture, you are really lost. There's two attitudes—yours and the airplane's ... relax, man, your legs are like iron on those rudders ... relax ... don't fight it ... make the airplane come to you ..."

Holding at a VOR was the worst for me. As the needles became more fidgety, I would cramp in more and more rudder until I was unwittingly holding reverse aileron. "Jim," I said, "this is a crooked airplane. It's kinked up somewhere and will not fly straight."

"Turn it loose a minute." I did, and it jumped sideways so far, I missed the whole VOR again. Shelton laughed out loud.

Missed approaches were not too bad, except for my fatal fixation on heading to the detriment of altitude.

I was also still plagued by occasional vertigo. Once on an approach to Galveston, Scholes Field did a slow roll right inside my head. Jim had said, "If I ever yell 'I got it!' I mean I got it. I'm not interested in finding out which of us is the strongest." He stopped the barrel roll and said, "If you ever get disoriented on approach, declare a missed approach and get the hell out. That other will kill you. A missed approach is for re-orientation. Never be too proud to go around."

I'll probably remember Shelton's ILS technique forever. "Your road is narrowing down to two and a half degrees on either side. Say those limits out loud to yourself if it helps, but leave those ailerons alone. Use rudders. Pedal it like a bicycle. And that glide slope is just like sliding down a slanted wire. If you're too slow, level out and gently fly into it again; if you're high, ease off a little power and let her sink a little."

I'd come down that chute babbling to myself, sweat trickling cold down my ribs, "two left, just two, that's all you get, wait for it, and you're low, hold level, and there it comes ... centers at 36 ... hold 36 ... and now you're high ..."

When the hair started to crawl on the back of my neck as the altimeter went below 250, Jim would flip up the hood and there it all lay, right where it was supposed to be, like the pathway to the Pearly Gates.

At this instant of transition to contact flying, Jim would lean forward, peer into my face and ask, "You alright?" I don't know what he was looking for, but I felt great. He varied between being a most gentle and sensitive instructor and the most infur- iating stress teacher, but a word of praise from him was worth the Medal of Honor to me. Once he flipped the hood and I found us in a bucketing crosswind. I painted one on and made the first intersection turnoff. He may have smiled, and I thought I heard him mutter, "Ain't no hill for a stepper."

After other flights, we would taxi to the ramp in sullen silence, and once he said, "You were so bad today I don't even want to talk to you about it." I regressed badly at about the two-thirds point, as I had in the simulator. The blowup came on an ILS approach when I reached for the mike to report "Outer marker, inbound." While I reached and talked, I swerved right, pegging the needle. Jim shouted, "Now what the hell did you do that for?"

Furious with myself as well as him, I yelled back, "Because I'm just a gahdamn student, that's why!" I overheard him telling this to Marsh later; both of them whooped a laugh.

These regressions brought another pride-crushing back-to-basics session. We flew the course without the hood. "So you can see what you have been visualizing." Then without a word, Jim took over the controls and began the most astonishing dem-onstration of routine flight that I have ever seen. The fly old master unwrapped his hidden stock of tricks and opened up my eyes to why professional pilots seem to be doing so little at the controls. He painted the needles in the center with almost imperceptible rudder movements. Went from approach speed to cruise speed and through altitude changes apparently using only the throttle. The last thing he ever touched was the trim wheel, and that just once. "Now you do it."

I copied his techniques and felt the tingle of having broken through to a subtle management of the airplane that I never knew was possible.

"Jim, why in hell didn't you show me all this from the beginning?"

"You weren't ready for it. Not deep enough into instrument flying to know that you needed it until now."

"Yessir."

It's funny; I always call him Jim on the ground, but calling him "sir" in the airplane seemed natural, too. Now I understood why.

><

One of the unexpected dividends awaiting you when you finally decide to don the plastic hood and find out what all the knobs on the panel are for is that you will enter into a level of flying proficiency that most VFR pilots don't even know exists.

January dissolved into February, and now I was so anxious to get it that I was over-trying. "Bax, you are worrying this airplane to death. Relax, man; you got a lot of bad habits to unlearn. I can force you to fly that panel with your eyes, but you are still listening VFR. You're flying partial panel. And quit ducking down to pick up those charts in a turn or one of these days you'll go snap-roll vertigo doing that ... and think ahead, man. Plan. Always consider your alternatives; so the VOR just flipped from 'to' to 'from' and the needle never centered? Well, what are you going to do now? Listen carefully, Baxter: When you are sitting up here in the gunk all by yourself, if you don't have a cold, deadly reason for doing some-thing—then don't do nothin'."

Fatigue, frustration and humiliation began to move in on me. Even if I ever learned to fly the insane perfection that these guys wanted, would I have the cods to actually bicycle down that beam someday, alone and blind, scared witless, knowing that the altimeter was going through 400 and there was solid earth down there in one minute more of this? Would I have it to go on down to the published 250? That one I still don't know, though I did it every day under the hood. I was pretty discouraged. Fed up, in fact.

A particularly shaggy approach at Galveston and the start of the long, butt-weary flight back to Hobby, concentrating on those slippery needles. Jim could sense how it was. Lit a cigarette and stuck it up under the hood on my lip. I slipped off my boots, wiggled my toes, unclamped my hands and decided he was probably the greatest guy in the world. The airplane flew better, too. But as for me, I was probably unteachable past a certain point we had already reached some time back.

Then one day I heard a chilling exchange over Houston Approach that wiped out any lingering doubts I may have had over the loss of "freedom of the skies" and my own sinking motivation. A Braniff captain on the ILS into Hobby reported in resigned tones, "There's a 150 playing around just under the clouds out here."

But for the random chance of a few seconds either way, that Boeing would have popped out of the cloud base on gauges and speared that happy VFR pilot in his little tin fish. The hell of it was they were both legal. The VFR pilot was clear of clouds and all that, but nothing required him to have an approach plate that would show him that he was playing in the middle of the busiest street in Houston, or be tuned to the approach frequency or even have his radio on.

><

I realized then that flying may be a great game, but it can only be survived by everybody knowing and playing by the same rules. Yet eight out of ten of the players are required to know only about one-fourth of the rules. Freedom of the skies be damned; this is madness.

><

I may become insufferable about this, like a reformed drunk busting into saloons and slapping the drinks out of everybody's hands, but for the first time in my life, I don't feel too guilty about calling myself a pilot in front of other pilots. With the ink still wet on my ticket, I'm no instrument pilot. (They said, "Here—now you have a license to go out and kill yourself.") But I'm working at it. And I have never worked so hard for, or been so proud of, anything in my life.

Getting there took from November 10, 1972 to February 10, 1973, and it didn't finish with any flourish of trumpets or garland of roses. At the low point of the sullen rides with Shelton, I was smitten with pneumonia. Two weeks of skulking around wondering if I was well or sick, and then I presented myself to Marsh's on a Saturday. I wasn't well, wasn't still sick, but any flying would be better than no flying. It seemed natural that the Old Man himself came gruffing out to ride with me; Saturday was Shelton's day off. "I don't like to shout in airplanes," was Marsh's only comment as we set sail to go crashing around the course.

On the home leg, he stirred himself out of his corner to pester me with a lot of irrelevant questions about what I'd do if this or that happened. He only stiffened up once when I almost pegged the needle on the localizer coming home. As I bicycled out of that one, I heard us both emit a long, shaky sigh.

Taxiing back to the ramp, he asked: "How do you think you did?"

"No better, no worse than usual, sir."

"Well, you just passed the check ride."

Chapter 3
The Newcomer

The low-time student pilot curves forward over the controls as if diminishing the inches between his nose and the windshield will bring the answer he is seeking a few moments sooner.

Within the past hour, he has found his way 50 miles beyond the horizon and successfully landed at a strange airport and located the men's room and then the coffee pot. Holding his cup with shaking hands, hoping no one would guess that this was his first cross-country solo.

Now, before him lie the fields of home, dappled in sun and shadow. The pasture where he hunted rabbits and looked up with longing at planes in the sky is passing below. Now it is he who has the view of the hawk. He wipes his palm on his thigh and reaches for the mike, rehearsing his speech. On the ground, he will play it like Ernie Gann said pilots are supposed to. He'll stroll in and hand over the keys and they will say, "Where have you been?"

And he will say, "Don't know. I was lost the whole time." And they will grin, and his heart will swell around the word inside his chest. "Pilot. Pilot. I am a pilot!"

Spring will be approaching as you lay aside this magazine, and if you are lucky and live in Nowheresville, as most of us do, you'll drive out to that little airport where you'll find an old building and an assorted group of very contented-looking men, perhaps a girl or two. They will ignore your arrival, so you must announce to no one, "Who do I talk to about learning to fly?" Conversation will cease, and they will turn and smile upon you warmly, and the hungriest-looking one of the lot will introduce himself and take you at once out to the airplane.

In time, you will come to know that there is a separate, distinct and never fully described social order that begins and ends at the edge of little airports. First, you will find a total honesty, found elsewhere only among small boats and men who take them to sea. The reasons for the honesty are the same: The element is hostile to the unfit men and vessels. They perish.

Secondly, you will find democracy as Jefferson dreamed of it. The night manager you couldn't even get an appointment to see will sit and talk with you for hours in the shade of the wing of his proud Bonanza.

And have you ever wondered who cures the doctor? You'll know when he invites you to come with him in his Mooney on his Tuesday off.

Finally, the neighborhood barn-raising spirit of frontier America still lives when the guy gets the cowling off his Piper and finds himself in a circle of eager eyes and willing hands.

So now you and the hungry-looking man are standing beside an innocent little Cessna. On this very first ride, you will be in the pilot's seat, and he'll be telling you the things you need to know as you need to know them. "Now first, this here is what we call the fuselage ..." In the beginning—even as it was told to him, years ago.

When you have descended from the skies on this first day, and on all the days thereafter, you will no longer be able to remember whatever it was that troubled you before you left the ground. And you will come to know that flying little airplanes from grass fields is, more than anything else, an experience in beauty.

Chapter 4
I Abort This Exam

Blew my commercial written exam, I did. Went right into the Flight Service Station and Pfft!

Oh, I thought I was ready, really ready. Ask me anything. Sit close to me and let me whisper FARs in your EAR. My mind was overstacked like a hay wagon to be gotten to market before it all blows away.

Not that I need a commercial ticket, understand. I was like Lucifer plunging from the heavens, powered only by flames of pride. I had been a private pilot since most of you were still wearing sleepers with feet in them. Private was enough to fly for fun. But private has lost a lot of its swagger. Private: as in piddle, Piper, puddles and putt putt putt. Ah, but to lean, the subject of the awed whisper, on the Coke machine, "He's a commercial pilot!"

They have a little side room for exams at the flight service station in Lake Charles, but there was a guy already in there, so they gave me the corner desk in the big room, the room with the radio, the radar and all those hanging sheaves of weather. The FAA men in white shirts were cordial and all that. There was a "good luck," and then we touched gloves and went to our corners to wait for the bell. The moment arrived and I became an Applicant for Written Exam on Government Soil.

With the confidence of the pure of heart, I unfolded my issued Phoenix Sectional and my 60 fourple-choice questionnaire. I hit the outer defenses running lightly on the balls of my mind. I knew the stuff alright, although the guy who phrased these questions didn't seem to have much of a grasp of it.

He kept giving me a choice of answers two of which were sheer folly and two utterly unworkable. I found myself wanting to help him along. I wanted to write in marginal comments, little essays of explanation to clear his head, but I would remember that no human would grade this sheet. It would be grazed over by a computer, curious only about whether my soft-lead pencil marks were in the proper parking slots. Defiantly, using body English, I tried to put meaning into each mark.

Then I discovered that I had left my plotter at home. I did have my Jepp chart PV-2 plotter, bristling with mileage scales, but if any of them fit on a sectional chart I never found out. Griped about this glitch, I rummaged up a Government envelope (penalty for private use, $300), hastily found a scale on the sectional and got 30 miles worth of pencil ticks across the top edge of the $300 envelope. But from there, nothing went right. Time-distance problems, fuel problems, none matched the choice of answers. In a light sweat, I reworked them, allowing for my boll weevil plotter, as the clock swallowed up another of the precious four allotted hours.

I began to feel a damp, rising sense of panic. Background noises filtered in. I could hear every pilot from Lafayette to Lake Charles, from Beaumont to Houston. It was a spanking clear day, and the FSS crew were evaluating the wits of each passing pilot by the number of gulps and gasps and fumbling sounds that came over the speakers. "A day like this and nobody needs us." All but some yo-yo out there who must have been beating his way westward at all of 60 knots. He went on forever, calling up each flight station, giving his life history and requesting a complete weather briefing every 50 miles. "He wants us to fly his plane for him." As a nonperson, I was overhearing the FSS in real life, like a man accidentally hidden in the ladies' rest room and listening to the girls compare dates. Some things, a man is a lot better off never hearing.

I grasped the horns of the test questions, leaving all the time and distance problems in the wreckage of my path. Visions of a 98 score became taunting yesterdays. Now, even the easy ones were wadding up in my mind. Everyone knows the cardinal altitudes for Visual Flight, but look how they worded this: measured from above ground level or above sea level? Okay, good for you, but according to magnetic heading or magnetic course? Treachery, I tell you, these questions are loaded with treachery.

All that exams of this type prove is that some men can comprehend an insurance policy. To learn by rote is to educate a fool. Why not let us sit at the feet of some good gray examiner who could probe our minds, who could draw forth and examine our store of knowledge? But then what would they do with the computer? I have a suggestion about what to do with the computer.

Things were deteriorating fast in my corner: Less than an hour to go and I was running out of time, out of confidence, out of tobacco. Then a school bus pulled up and unloaded 40 children and four brass-mouthed teachers. A tour!

"Oh, lookee the big green tee vee screen!"

"Where do you keep the airplanes?"

"Why is the old man over in the corner crying? Why is his head in the ashtray?"

They left. I still had 20 questions and only 20 minutes to go. No way. I quit.

"Sir, I abort this exam."

Shocked silence.

"Well, Bax, you can't just abort. It ain't like a missed approach. You either pass or fail."

"Then I fail."

In sympathetic silence, he gathered up my papers. I explained about no plotter and nothing coming out right and showed him where I had copied the scale. As gently as possible, my friend explained that I had copied the scale of the Phoenix area inset, and that the real scale is at the bottom of the chart. And if I had only asked for it, there was a Weems plotter right in that middle drawer.

Out in the sparkling sunshine, I wanted to go right up to that Cessna and kick it in the side. Tear up my license. Catch a bus. Or a social disease.

I sulked a week. Wouldn't even go out to the airport. Went down to the depot and watched the trains come in. Engineers don't have to navigate; you ever think of that? For me, they should put flanges on airplane tires.

Later, I went to mean ol' Bob Marsh's flying school at Houston Hobby Field. I crawled in, enduring their scoffs and jeers while they strapped the books to my back and shackled me to a desk. Three days later, Bob signed off my 40 grade and pulled a 78 in the Houston exam office. Ain't much, but it beats 69.

All this stuff is just alibis. Truth is, I wasn't ready.

Chapter 5
Unpadded Cell

This is one of those hair-raising stories that you know will turn out all right in the end. I didn't know that at the time, though, and man, oh man, what a ride.

I had launched from home plate on the Gulf Coast of Texas, to fly the coastal crescent, fuel stop at Mobile, then on to Florida in 27 November, my 1968 Mooney with the faded orange paint, 180 engine, hand-fired gear and more King Instrument Flight Rules stuff than the hull is worth. With me were my two teenage daughters, both of whom think the ol' man is neat, and who will trample each other for a chance to make a trip—any trip—with me. All that is as good as it can get, thank you very much.

The Flight Service Station briefer spoke of a stalled cold front on that early winter morning. The front, one of the first that would freeze you poor Yankees' behinds, reached from the Great Lakes down into Tennessee and was influencing weather along the coast by backing up some warm tropical air masses that were trying to get ashore. The forecast said that I would break out of the clouds about halfway to New Orleans, encounter scattered layers and showers, then fly into steadily improving weather. My "aw shucks, you know better than that" feeling was confirmed as we continued through solid but stable cloud and light rain beyond New Orleans. A good standard westerly was giving us the coveted three miles per minute, and I was enjoying the gray and doing a pretty professional job.

><

I had been lollygagging along, expecting sunshine, and hadn't done my usual rehearsal with the Jepp plates. Radar was already turning me for the interception and giving me descents when I was flipping pages in the book. Not good. It was a wiggle-waggle approach, and the cloud had turned that deep-green bottom-of-the-sea color that means you are near the ground when the lights appeared, right between a wiggle and a waggle. The kids said I sure was good. Yeah. Heh, heh, heh.

Mobile FSS advised me of continued low ceilings down into central Florida, strong southerly winds and a sigmet for turbulence below 7,000, but with a flourish of satisfaction, the briefer pointed out that I would be well clear of the cold front, which was moving a little now but was still north of us. Not a word about a warm front, and me too dumb to recognize it.

Mobile had gone down with fog and light rain. I enjoyed taxiing out past that dead-still flight line for a just about zero-zero takeoff. A few landing lights, zip, zip, and we were on the gauges.

I had filed for 9,000 to top the reported turbulence. They cleared me for 7,000, and I settled down to holding about 25 degrees right drift. It was really blowing but still smooth. Then near Gleet Intersection, the man at JAX Center said he was painting a little heavy weather across my course. Did I want radar vectors? Sure, I need all the help I can get since I quit flying railroads and water tanks.

Right 10 degrees didn't do much more than ooch me back onto the centerline; that invisible wind was really pouring in. Gleet is between Destin and Panama City, north of both. That's the last place I knew where I was for a long time. At Gleet, I drove right into the freight elevator.

It didn't start out with a wham; in fact, there were only one or two whams all the way through, but each was like lifting the Mooney about 20 feet and dropping it on the ramp. We whooshed right up at about 2,000 feet per minute, then in less than a minute, we were headed down at 2,000 fpm. No warning. Usually if you hit an embedded cell in the daytime, the cloud color changes to dark blue or bile green; this one just went darker gray. It was like trying to fly up a fire hose. I would never have dreamed an airplane could swallow that much water.

I was still pretty cool. Then we flew into the inner chambers, and I felt ice cold in my guts. It all took place in less time than I need tell it. JAX was on the horn trying to tell me something, my back-seat daughter, who had been stretched out asleep loose from her belt, was hitting the cabin roof, and the Jepp book was beating us badly up front. "Grab that thing," I yelled at the front-seat kid, who was hanging by one hand, clutching the door strap, legs and arms flying. She looked like a rodeo rider.

Suddenly I realized that the rate-of-climb needle was all the way over, and I didn't know whether it had gotten there climbing or diving. We hit the hail and shocks that blurred the rest of the panel. I don't know why, but I started putting it all on the tape at JAX Center. I've been a broadcaster all my life; I guess doing a play-by-play of our own disaster afforded me some small measure of sanity.

"JAX, 27 November is in a cell. I am getting over 2,000-fpm changes both ways, heavy rain and hail."

"Daddy, I'm going to be sick!" The daddy instinct is strong. I laid a comforting hand on the kid in back, dumped out sandwiches and Fritos and gave her the empty bag. When I turned back to the panel, the horizontal situation indicator looked as though it was tumbling.

"Marginal control of the aircraft, JAX, one passenger sick, the cabin is in a shambles, am reducing power ..."

Maneuvering speed is 132, but I had no idea what our airspeed was because the needle was swinging. Gear-out speed is 120, but us old hand-operated manual-gear Mooney owners know that it will stand whatever it takes.

Slowing down and dropping the wheels quieted the spearing lunges at sky and earth. Now the Mooney just whipped and floated like a leaf at a windy corner. Then the engine quit. Ice!

"... and partial power failure, JAX, unable to hold altitude or maintain normal attitude. Falling through 5,500." All on the tape.

In the seconds it took for that little Lycoming to drink all the ice water melting out of the carbure-tor, the prop seemed to flick still for an instant. I knew by now that I was in a fight for life. An attempt at a 180 would be suicide. JAX had taken the friendly concerned attitude of an old uncle at the deathbed. "You'll be out of it soon." But when that prop ticked, with us falling and flipping and the hail roaring, the little darling in the front seat leaned over to the daughter in back, and, in a voice sweet as Tinker-bell's, said, "Oh shi-yut."

She said it so calmly, and my kids never talk that way in front of Dad. I felt a well of laughter bubble up in me, got the out loud giggles looking at that surprised little pug-nosed freckled face. That made the whole day. Everything outside was still going to pieces, but something had changed inside me. I put on my Ernie Gann face, heard the engine pick up its full hearty roar, remembered that the

Mooney wing is made in one piece and that I have never heard of one breaking up in the air, whispered thanks to old Al Mooney and settled down to fly right on out of there.

We never did break out of cloud, but there was no doubt when we flew out of the cell. I told JAX they'd better clear me for 5,000 because that's where I was, and man, don't send anybody else through here.

We fought headwinds down past Cross City and scud halfway across Florida before we saw orange groves, lakes and sunshine.

But let me tell you something. When that briefer tells you where the cold front is, and you see those wind shifts and rain to the south, ask about the warm front, too. It'll eat your lunch.

Chapter 6
Conversation Piece

The language between pilots and controller must be swift and clear, a ritualistic exchange that by its very nature creates a perfect stage for occasional humor or pathos.

Once, on a busy weekend, I heard St. Louis Center ask the pilot of a Cardinal RG for his ground-speed.

"One-sixty-one knots," sweetly sang the wheels-up Cessna.

There was a deliberate, drawn-out silence for about a five count; then St. Louis drawled, "Aw, c'mon." And a score of amused pilots heard St. Louis haggle the proud new owner of the RG down to 141 knots.

I got an unexpected name call once in the congested Dallas TCA (traffic collision avoidance system). I had encountered cloud, filed en route, got cleared for 3,000 and was a little flustered copying clearances and getting my IFR (instrument flight rules) senses settled down.

A deep voice said, "Hang in there, Bax." I looked across to my wife in surprise, and she said, "Bill," recognizing the voice of a mutual friend she had flown with during her stewardess years.

I picked up the mike and said, "Bill?" and the mystery voice said, "Come up a hundred feet and ride in the sunshine." My rudder must have been cutting the cloud surf like a shark's fin. Fort Worth let us get away with all that.

Sometimes the system nearly breaks down in the search for official terminology to cope with hard-to-describe situations. Houston Hobby was having a busy day, mixing the swarm of general aviation with a Braniff 727 whistling inbound through the smog.

HUD—Ah, Braniff, there seems to be an object which is moving on the active ... It seems to be, ah, a small cow ... a heifer.

BI (not concealing obvious mirth)—Ah, roger, copy heifer on the active.

Then somebody mooed into his mike, and there was more laughter until HUD came in with, "Aw right you guys. Cut that out."

At least one airline, whose name I won't mention so as to protect those obviously rotten with guilt, has developed the highly secret "800 code." This is a list of things you always wanted to say back, but in language acceptable only in a Marine Corps mortar squad. But as such things tend to do, the 800 code has leaked to centers, so when a line captain vents his frustration at an awkward approach, set up by replying "815—(B.F.D.)," center may come back with an 816—(hang it in your ear).

What I have sometimes wished for is a code way to tell a controller I'd like to send him a bottle of Scotch. As in the time Chicago was swamped with traffic and prowling thunderstorms, and I hit an imbedded cell while in solid cloud. As the hail hit the windshield, the Jepp charts hit the roof and my heart hit my boots. What I wanted to do was yell, "He-e-elp! Get me out of this!" But with that perverse pride of dying pilots, I held off the wing-bending panic and said something official, like, "Ah, Chicago. Twenty-Seven November is in heavy precip, hail, turbulence and lightning. I will accept any reasonable suggestion."

Chicago, whoever he is, and may his shadow never decrease, laid aside his other traffic, got an ident and after a deliberate scope-searching pause, advised me to come left to 90 degrees and said "You ought to be out of that in three minutes."

After exactly three minutes of being grateful that Al Mooney had designed the wing spar in one solid chunk from tip to tip, I burst streaming out of the well of it and into light air. Before I could report, Chicago called me and quipped, "Seemed like three years, didn't it." That's when I needed the "I will send you a bottle of Scotch" code.

Now here are two instances of the most ruthless disregard for a pilot in trouble.

As the 1975 Reading Air Show ended and the great exodus of aircraft began, I was among those in the full cabin of a scheduled de Havilland Twin Otter commuter airliner. A ground delay developed, and much twitching spread among the passengers about missing connecting flights.

The young skipper of the Otter was obviously in on whatever was happening, listening intently on his headset. So I leaned forward from my front-row seat and told him that his load consisted of nothing but licensed pilots, so he might as well let us in on it and forego the usual airline song about something being wrong.

The pilot looked back at us, groaned, shrugged and fed Reading Approach into the cabin speakers. The delay was a real emergency: a VFR pilot, lost and trapped on top between layers, blocking hundreds of IFR departures from Reading. The response to one pilot's hour of terror from 18 of his fellow birdmen on the ground was calloused braying. "Oh what a yo-yo!" "I hope he runs out of gas before I miss my connection." "He should, he's been up there lost for 40 minutes now. He's got to fall out soon."

I presume this luckless aviator was vectored to sunnier skies; at least, I never read about him in papers.

The other incident is unfortunately typical of over-crowded airspace and over-loaded controllers, a system that must grind on, and woe to the halt and the lame who get in its pathway.

A 310 pilot at 8,000 in cloud broke in on New York Center with a report of heavy ice and an immediate altitude-change request. New York, up to his ears in traffic, gave him a cold "stand by." Two pilots at lower altitudes cut in and reported no ice at four and at six. New York, who had the unfortunate grating accent of a Manhattan cabbie, cracked down on the Good Samaritans with a rulebook reminder about improper use of the radio for personal communications. Our pilot growled to himself, "Why that creep! Watch for traffic—it will be 310 dropping through encased in a solid block of ice."

><

In contrast to the cold hard world of the metropolitan skies, where they say "G'day," and it sounds neither good nor day, there is the easy midnight mood down in the warmer climes, where there are long stretches of silence on the graveyard shift and the pilots use the romantic "S'long." I usually say, "Thank y'all."

Here, over vast mid-America, the night-mail pilot and controller come to recognize each other, and a terminal forecast may include some ball scores and where the bass are hitting. I know of one grizzled corporate jet jock—and so do the Feds—whose call sign within 50 miles of home plate is to ring his cow bell over the mike.

Richard L. Collins courts the rare thrill of personal recognition in his name-branded Cessna Skyhawk "40RC." Collins' watchdog vendetta about the proliferation of controllers is widely known among the boys in the towers. So at Oshkosh '75 I met a controller on the ground who said, "We had your buddy, Collins, in here yesterday. The gun was in place, but we were real busy and he got off before anybody could find the clip."

As the skies get fuller and the radar gets better, we feel ever more the close, hot breath of the controller over our shoulders, even out where VORs and filling stations are 100 miles apart. I always blush and smart when some radar voyeur tells me and the rest of the world that I'm four miles south of the centerline. Back in the good ol' days, sloppy flying could be just a personal thing.

And in some areas, I'm hearing a new, devastating phrase that the ATC uses to herd some drifting pilot along. They say, "Where are you going?"

That is so bad. It implies that the course keeper is so hopelessly mixed up that radar is no longer certain of which city he is aiming at. I'm still trying to think up a real good flange-him-up reply to that one.

Chapter 7
Islands in the Sun

Many strange, wonderful creatures inhabit that shadowy zone where land, sky and sea meet and wash together. They adapt to this shifting shoreline, each finding the narrow band in which he can survive. They feed upon each other and migrate unknowingly, answering some eons-old timetable, guided by a mysterious sense of direction. They are the rock louse, the phantom crab, the big-eyed gobie.

More recent evolution has added the vee-tail Bonanza, the straight-legged Piper, the svelte-winged Cessna. These are hard-shelled, winged creatures that are capable of brief periods of noisy but spectacular flight. Their migration from Northeastern America to the Bahaman Islands lasts but one week, the signal for their swarming coming when ice forms over the bridges in New Jersey and the snow is navel deep in Montreal.

Their rallying cry is "Bahamas Treasure Hunt," a call heard only during harmless blizzards of brightly colored pamphlets borne northward on trade winds from the Bahamas Ministry of Tourism. The call sets up an itch in the wallet so irresistible that many creatures make the arduous migration repeatedly. This year, the flock was so thick that many were turned back at the shoreline; all the roosting trees were full.

Since all of these birds are land creatures, there is a great ceremony prior to their launching from the continental edge outward over 60 miles of relentless ocean. They flock into such favored sanctuaries as Tilford's and Dan Darling's, where their pockets are emptied and their aircraft filled with bright yellow flotation objects. The purpose of those objects is to prolong drowning should one of those flimsy little wires come loose.

The flock quiets its nervous clackings by the dipping of beaks in alcohol. This is a quaint custom by which its members can later be identified any-where among the island roosts. They depart at daybreak, flying forward but looking backward and crying "omigod omigod" until they can see land no more.

In the Bahamas, the natives are noted for their great sense of humor. Their wit is dry and droll, and an outstanding example of it was in naming one roosting spot "Freeport." There is nothing free in Freeport. Freeport is a city on the Grand Banana Island, a fact that comes as a shock to most of the flock, who thought the whole area was named Nassaus (from the Grecian Emperor Nassaus, who threw up at orgies). The flock roosts noisily together in Freeport at the Royal Pilfer Hotel, gets one last chance to show off its expensive luggage and then is scattered to the Doubt Islands.

The quaint Doubt Islands got their name because of doubt over whether they actually existed. Columbus discovered the first Doubt Island and named it San Salvador, which means, "Thank God we found something out here." But when he got back home, people doubted his story. Same thing still happens.

Doubt about the islands also exists in the hearts of the treasure-hunting birds as they leave a coastal departure point flying low enough to look for clues and find nothing but sea in the direction of the next island. They do have migratory aids, of course. One is a Jepp chart that has so many compass-rose marks on it that it has finally reached the point of being totally unintelligible. There is another chart, furnished by the flock leaders and The Minister. Just where you need them, it has no compass roses at all. But on the back, there is a comforting message from Bahamas Minister Maynard to read while you fly a blind heading wishing you had asked someone about the wind.

Those feeling the block of panic rising in the throat can call up Nassau Radio, whose frequency is improperly listed on the Treasure Hunt chart in order to create an eerie silence and perpetuate that legend of mysterious radio failures in the Bermuda Triangle. Some will find the correct frequency—it's only two clicks away—but no clue-exchanging, please. Once you reach Nassau Radio, they will give you a squawk code, though there is no radar for little birds down low. As you talk to Nassau, you can hear calypso music and laughter in the background, and that is a comfort. I envisioned a limbo contest going on at Center and said to myself, "Why should I be an uptight American and miss all the fun?"

I was still laughing and singing when I found the Island of Urethra. What matter that I was aiming at Greater Eczema. We are only here to have fun. I tossed my treasure map and all its pesky clues away, as most do by the second day. Why not? Now that you are there, who needs the excuse anymore?

There are 700 of these islands scattered over 100,000 square miles of crystal-clear ocean, but the total population is smaller than that of Houston. Nicer, too. There are no two islands alike, though the trend is that the eastern fringe is more New England coast, with rocky limestone cliffs, and the western group is more South Seas, with crescent beaches of warm sand and swaying tall palms. The names are quaint. Bimini was named for the sound of steel drums, which on a clear night you can hear from Miami. Small Hope Bay was named from what Morgan said to Teach after they buried their treasure there, slaughtered the crew and were rowing back to the ship: "Small hope of seeing any of that again." Hard Bargain Bay was named for a man who had the plugs changed in his Cessna 172 there.

There are services available in the Bahamas. The Bahamas have, in fact, always existed by the ready availability of services. The first trade route from the early Colonies was a triangle of rum, sugar and slaves between Georgia, Africa and the Bahaman Islands. The place has always been handy for operations that others needed to conduct but not close to the house. The Queen based her pirates there and later sold Enfield muskets to the Confederacy via the Bahamas. There was rum during Prohibition and gambling today, and the future is trending toward tuck-away banking. In the Bahamas, you are never far from an airport or a bank. Good thing, too.

And in these islands, I found my own island paradise, to which I shall return as soon as I finish this story. It is right out of Michener and *Tales of the South Pacific.* I will not name it but will let you hunt for it. That lets me tell the story without clinging to the facts.

The Viking founded my paradise 16 years ago. He had reached the male menopause and did not like who he was or what he did. Casting free of briefcase, wife and kiddies, he came to this place of clear seas and crescent beaches. Still suicidal, he strapped himself, an observer and 100 pounds of stone to a plank and shot frothing down to 462 feet, setting an unofficial scuba record and experiencing every known human emotion in those five minutes. He survived, vowed never to do that again and began building stone-and-wood lodges.

Years passed, and a luxurious yacht put in with Mr. Rocks and his lovely, bored wife, Ms. Vassr. Six days elapsed. Ms. Vassr announced to her hubby, who was *so* busy with his vast toys, "Dear John, this terminates my part of the cruise and our union." Today, she is the Viking's wife, and the heart and intellect of the place.

It is a spot where you forget your shoes and watch after the first day, and the kitchen help and boat hands come sit at the table with you. Air-conditioning is by trade winds, television is the tidal rock pools, great books and brave ideas come in the still nights.

Our treasure hunt ended there. There was hugging and weeping when we left. I dipped low with orange wings flashing in the sun, looked long and thought of what one island philosopher told me: "You can use it all up, but you can't take none of it home with you."

There are many strange and wondrous creatures that survive in this ever-changing band between sea, water and air. The female horseshoe crab comes ashore, dragging her mate along. The whelks cruise for clams at the gaming tables, wrap a muscular foot around their trophy and rasp out a neat hole with their radula to extract the succulent meat inside. The Bahamas have always existed by the ready and cheerful availability of services.

And the place is only 30 minutes away in a Cessna 172.

Chapter 8
Big Sky

My throat was full of wanting to go home—to see my own familiar patch, my dog in my lane. It was a thousand miles or more from Oshkosh down to the curve of the Gulf of Mexico, so I went out to the field and touched my airplane. Walked all around her and asked if she was ready to vault the broad belly of this nation. One does not lightly mount the step and ask the little engine to run eight hours, or close one's mind to what nuts and bolts may have shaken off during the night. Even though cars do it all the time, pulling off to the side of the road in a little airplane nearly always gets your picture in the papers.

Oshkosh fell below at 10 minutes after nine in the morning and became a memory. I took off my shoes and leaned back to the soft rumble of the cruise setting for 1,500 feet and set a course line for Janesville, wherever that is. The airplane was strong and steady; my heart was full of the freedom of flight. I was low enough to see what was in a pickup truck, to tell how old the kids were by the wash on the line, to see the green richness of Wisconsin and the fat cattle always facing the wind. Little clear lakes kept coming up in surprise, piers stepped out over the water from shaded homes on the shore.

And this must be Illinois; it's changed. The first settlers here had time to lay out the section lines, and the roads run to the squares. Mile after mile of these squares, rich in crops, and in each square, the little quadrangle of trees that shade the house, barn and silo. I wondered how it looks from down there living in that sea of grain with only the distant silo to break the flat horizon.

><

I wondered about the details of life under each farm roof. Was there love in there or desperation? Were they sitting across the corner of the table not speaking, getting nothing but bad news and crime shows on TV? How I wish they could see from here.

Sometimes the scars of factory sites slid beneath my wings, but even the cities were dwarfed and all their suburban dottings made small by the limitless prairie sea. And the Interstate system that looms so large from your car is only a faint etching. The land doesn't make the press wires or the nightly dispatches except in dry commodity figures, but it lies out there in the silver looping of broad rivers. The land reaches a thousand miles in any direction, the pattern of slow tractor wheels, the careful tending of a man's hand slowly pumping its life toward the screaming cement of the Las Vegases, New Yorks and LAs.

I flew enchanted, held in the bright crystal of sunlight. Midday heat baking up from the fields jostled my wings, then settled into the cockpit to stay. The course line to Capitol's beacon lay right over the dome of the old Gothic statehouse of Missouri. Harry Truman and hanging judges. In the distance, the purple folds of the Boston Mountains promised Arkansas.

Better not stretch it the extra 100 miles to Little Rock, because the tanks are getting light and I'm getting a little crazy and want to embrace all those people and paint murals in their post offices and tell them how great they are.

So tip back the wings and hello, Walnut Ridge, Arkansas. Half way. Inside the old-pilot-scuffed building, the delightful surprise of a little calico-curtain restaurant and a sloe-eyed girl who brought me a hamburger right off the grill.

It felt like it should have been more than half way. I had spent myself in the glories back there. Now the sun was hot brass in the windshield and the legs between VORs were 100 miles or more. I picked up a freeway that looked like it went to Little Rock and cheated along that until a big blue thunderstorm woke up and nudged me out of its pasture.

Now the country was pines and red gullies and desperate little strip towns and a newer breed of man, who has much to learn about his stewardship. He was out there bulldozing great swaths of the forest and laying bare more reddening gullies. I tried not to hate him until he learns. And I sneaked past Little Rock without breaking my long silence on the radio, but I listened and heard them talk about me. "Traffic, southwest heading, altitude unknown."

The 100 miles or so down to Shreveport took about a month, and that little airplane and I squirmed and sweated until we didn't have anything that fitted each other anymore. Oh, how I wanted Shreveport. Shreveport is almost home. From there, it's all downhill. I decided I'd better work Shreveport Approach, but working the radio meant breaking the spell, letting the ground people in. The song was ended.

The heat had fried my radios as well as my brains. It was 95 degrees in the cockpit. Shreveport Approach talked some gibberish until I was able to squeeze out of their grasp, and then I was alone again.

It's nearly all lakes south out of Shreveport, lakes and cool water and bass boats in shaded coves. May the Corps of Engineers fry in hell for wanting to pave the rivers, but these lakes are their masterpiece. Manmade lakes, so huge that they show up in photographs made from halfway to the moon. A bittersweet tradeoff: the old truck patch farmstead buried beneath the waters for a place in the sun where its children's children can play.

And then the sawmill stacks of home were coming up, and yonder lay a gap in the forest— Eastex's secret strip, smooth concrete known only to the jet of Time, Inc. I could see my own sandbar down there, Village Creek, waiting for me, to bathe away the day in the shade of her willows. Pappy came up on the Unicom and told me Diane was waiting with a Mason jar of something full of ice, and at 10 minutes to six, I taxied up to waiting arms.

><

I have lived when a trip of 50 miles meant the entire day, counting waiting for the river ferries and changing a tire on the old Dodge a time or two.

But Daddy didn't mind; it was so much better than the horse of his childhood. He said we were lucky—that the car would change our lives.

Now I live in an age when a man who works for wages can own a small airplane and in one day unfurl the width of this continent and see things that Carl Sandburg and Thomas Wolfe could only dream of.

Chapter 9
The Flying Goofball

The pilot was of middling years and instrument rated, and so was his rented Cessna 172. What he did was to almost run it out of gas in the middle of an instrument flying night over the wooden swamplands of southwest Louisiana.

Had he run it dry, he would have been memorialized in one of those endless reports that say, "Almost one out of five accidents resulting from engine failure is caused by fuel starvation." Among other things lost in the wreckage would have been the record of what was going on inside his head during his last minutes.

He arrived at home plate safely, though shaken by the experience, and, in the cold light of dawn, felt compelled to share with me his innermost thoughts, dwelling not so much on what had happened, but why. He seemed dismayed by the awareness of something within himself that was both alien and deadly and recognized that his experience with peril had been almost planned and that the telling of it was part of the payoff. His choice of words, his body language and shining eyes confirmed it.

Beneath the light dusting of contrition there was an "Oh wow, look at me!" He was aware of that, too, as he told of how he passed up opportunities to reduce or eliminate the danger until, at last, his escape opportunities and his chances of making it had both diminished to a point of equal nothingness. At this time, he began to experience some total emotion, a natural high, of which only a part was fear and a sense of his own frail mortality.

"I want to tell you this while I'm still pringling over it," he said, and told how his jaded navcom set would either nav or com but would not do both at the same time and how he could have avoided all this anyway from the outset by purchasing gas.

"They told me the gas man had gone home for supper, but there was an emergency number if I needed him. Who wants to call an 'emergency' when he's used only an hour and a half out of four hours' worth of fuel? So I broke one of my own rules: never miss a chance to gas up."

He described his parting form the small circle of friends at the airport. "We all felt the mood at the dark and spooky airport—the cold metal of the plane, the night utterly black—but only one of the guys' dates felt it enough to say it. 'Y'all be careful, hear?' she said. 'I'm always careful hon,' said I. 'These things scare me to death.' "

He said his first concern was getting settled down for the transition to instrument flight. Then he found an airways intersection that afforded a good check point for working a time-and-distance problem. He was bucking a 30-knot headwind but never realized it until he worked out the actual groundspeed for himself. Seventy knots! He worked it again, and it came out the same. Until then, the gas gauges weren't even on his instrument panel; now they loomed big as watermelons.

He worked out a time-and-distance problem to home. It matched exactly his fuel on board—no reserve. Just 20 minutes away, but well to the left of his course line, lay a large metropolitan airport, but he held his heading for home, thinking, "Jesus, I've never done a fool thing like this before."

Fifty miles from home, and with both gauges sunken into their final quadrant (they seemed to rush there), he contacted Air Traffic Control and was advised that he was 15 minutes late on his flight plan, that the weather was good there, but the gas sellers were gone for the night.

"I pictured the hassle of trying to get a rental car, a room or driving home and back. But you know, I really wanted to try it, to tough it out. Get home-itus? Partly. Deadly game of wits? Yes, some."

><

As he left the last lighted airport behind, he learned that surface winds were only seven knots and variable, so he asked for minimum low altitude. He was cleared for 1,500 feet, but knowing the terrain was empty, he descended to 1,000—and became a third-degree open-freestyle player at the wits game.

"I throttled back to 2,200 and leaned that Lycoming down so far that it occasionally reached back and banged on the firewall with its fist. But those gas gauges froze. They ceased to move. I decided I must have figured out a way to refine and manufacture fuel in flight. Then I got the cold colly-wobbles, real ones: one thousand feet in the mists, over the trees and alligators. This was no game; I could really get killed doing this. I felt humble."

He figured he had a total of four hours' endurance in the Cessna 172. By the time he had been in the air three hours and 50 minutes, home plate radar contacted him, and he learned he was 11 minutes from the threshold. He advised them of the situation and flew the remaining miles enjoying their undivided and most solicitous attention, while letting his mind leap through broken cloud from one forced-landing site to the next in the city below.

When he topped off the tanks upon arrival, he learned that he had 4.5 gallons usable on board when he reached the ramp. He had learned that one can use low power settings to trade speed for endurance, but now he wanted to find out why he had done it. "This is how people run out of gas, but why me?"

><

Because I suspected this sort of behavior is more common than any of us would like to admit, I called the Civil Aeromedical Institute of the FAA offices in Oklahoma City for a most revealing conversation with one of the flight surgeons there. I told him the story.

"What you say is not surprising. We have solid figures that one-third of the fatalities in general aviation accidents originate from irresponsible acts. Flying under bridges, chasing coyotes, buzzing beaches, landing on the road for a beer, flying through the arch at St. Louis—suicidal stuff. These are problems dealing with human psychological makeup, and we have no psychiatrist on our staff. In fact, there are only nine health conditions that we can refuse a medical certificate for, and that amazes aviation people from other countries. We know there are behavior patterns that can reveal this sort of individual, and we have considered asking the DOT to let us use a person's traffic-safety records for early-screening purposes; but that smacks of Big Brother watching you, a sort of invasion of privacy.

The FAA medic then mentioned that a computer cross-check is made on reported accidents and that repeaters may get a friendly visit from the local accident-prevention counselors, but the nature of the visit can only be advisory. He spoke wistfully of having flight instructors act as an early screen to weed out the immature or emotionally unstable students, but there is no plan to do that. The FAA does get a rich input of data on the application for any airman's medical certificate, if you volunteer your background of dizziness, nervous trouble, drug or narcotic habit, excessive drinking, attempted suicide, your traffic convictions or other brushes with the law. The local medical examiner is asked to note any "personality deviation." My FAA spokesman made no mention of what, if any, use is made of this information. He did say, however, that they are aware of the use of the airplane for suicide, real no-note suicides, that get chalked up with the accident statistics.

The FAA seems to be aware of, but powerless to deal with, the flying goofball.

This is not to say that pilot attitude as a contributing factor in accidents has gone unnoticed in aviation medicine. The FAA doctor talked about Dr. Gibbons, formerly with the FAA in Fort Worth and now with the City and County Health Division of Salt Lake City, who has done research into actual suicides by aircraft.

He also said that the Navy conducts an after-the-crash study called a psychological autopsy. Dr. Roger Reinhart has attempted to establish behavior patterns by reconstructing those pieces of the pilot's psyche that might have contributed to the crash, much as the FAA today reconstructs pieces of the airplane. And the Feds have a man in Washington, Dr. Robert Yanowitch, a psychologist and a pilot with the Office of Aviation Medicine, who is researching along the same lines but has no way to implement his findings yet.

My FAA spokesman also mentioned a committee of 28 psychiatrists from the ranks of the Flying Physicians who are urging psychological testing to screen out the immature and unstable pilot applicants, but the FAA medic added wistfully, "It would cost money."

The FAA public-affairs officer worded it differently: "We haven't overly worked this aspect."

><

Back to our hero of the night skies, who seemed to be speaking from two minds. "I was playing a delightful, secret and dangerous game, and I really wonder why. I presented the story to my wife that night as a tale of my great skill and nerve, without which my precious body would have been strung out in the trees. Human behavior is very much a part of flying, but I never heard or read a word about it during all my instruction as a student. Why?"

Well, I am in no way qualified to enter into the bushes of psychology, but I have lived for half a century and been around airplanes and pilots a lot of that time. The very personality traits that make for a dangerous pilot in today's cabin planes and closely gridded skies were, it seems, the same forces that drove those early pioneers who carried aviation forward out of its unsafe and unprofitable infancy of biplanes and barnstorming. With boots and jodhpurs, they set themselves apart from the common crowd, lowered the level in the brandy bottle, then set it in the cockpit as an artificial horizon; they brought in the mail, laughing at the night's storm.

The heritage of the macho pilot is waning now, as any frontier yields to the homesteaders. On any Saturday, a man in a tie and jacket will teach you to fly a civilized airplane in a civilized manner; but down at the saloon, if you could sit in the corner with a group of good, gray airline captains off-duty, you would sometimes hear the same hair-curling tales of narrowly missed disasters that you hear back in your hangar.

Not one element of the aviation community is willing to admit any of this to outsiders; with the exception of the air shows, where it belongs, flying for the hell of it has gone underground. And that, I suppose, is some small measure of progress.

Chapter 10
The Big Sweat

I need to share this one with you while the hair, hide and hooves are still on it. While the sweat of it is not yet washed off and precludes, through our covenant, the reckless lying of survivors, the bravado of tomorrow. I have just made my first really low approach: "300 feet, one-quarter mile and fog, sky obscured, runway visibility range 4,000 feet. ... Did you copy the weather, Niner-Six-Zero?"

Do you want to drink of this cup? Are you aware? Are you sure this is what you want to enter into? Oh, gentle tower man. Later, after you had held me like a mother holds a tiny babe in arms and crooned to me, and I was rolling and alive on cement, you did tell me that at the moment of my touchdown, the sky had lowered still more and what we really had was 200 feet, and the lowest decision height that I can find on the plate for Beaumont-Port Arthur, Jefferson County is 216 feet (200). Oh, lordy.

Understand, I did not overtly bargain for this. My personal decision height is 800 feet and one mile, because I am green and an amateur at this, and until this day there were many important things yet unresolved in my mind. But overriding it all was the simple fact that low approaches really scare hell out of me. And, until I contacted Beaumont Approach at Honey Intersection, still on top in the dying brightness of the sun, I was expecting 800 and four. I got it in writing, from the flight service station at my departure point, just two hours ago at Love, Dallas.

There was that business of Houston air traffic control, who was one of those garglers who sat too close to the mike and ripped off all his lingo like we were all Delta captains with Collins flight directors to pave the way and one good man with nothing more to do than listen closely on a high-powered radio and try to make English out of what he was spouting.

This Houston ATC got peeved with me because the Cessna was slow and rented and I was not high-keyed to the fact that Niner-Six-Zero was me. How could he know that what I was doing was putting on my buckler and my shield and preparing to do battle when my moment of truth would come in that white ice cream below? My mind was often far away. And once, when he got churlish with me, I got churlish with him; in my most easy Texican, I asked, "Hewston, cain't you talk like thi-yus?" It was chancy, but it cooled his machine gun some.

When he handed me off to Beaumont Approach, we were both thinking good riddance.

And when Beaumont let me down into the stuff, I decided this was not the time for false pride and to take this man to my warm side and tell him how it really is. "Beaumont, take me slow. This will be the lowest approach I ever made." And that's when I felt the humanness of the man in the cement tower peering into his green scope at the man in the fragile aluminum who was about to bet his old arse and all of its fixtures. He took me slow.

><

Let me tell you now and tell all the high honchos of the FAA who this man is. He is Glen Martinka. I never met him, never pressed the flesh, but for a while tonight, we were brothers.

Glen took me down to 2,500 and then down to 1,500, and in my mind's eye, I could see all the refineries and their tall stacks super-imposed on the opaque grayness ahead. Glen kept calling out targets to me—yes, there was other traffic. An Air Force Herky bird was over here sharpening the blade of skill against the stone of danger. And unbelievably, there was some klutz out in a Grumman Traveler shooting approaches. Jerry's Aviation. Whoever it was, they must have cods to carry in a wheelbarrow to go play on a day like this. "Beaumont, thanks for the traffic reports, but I can't even see my own wing tips."

And Metro went barreling out for Houston, ho hum, just another day. Pros, those guys, pea patch pros, the great captains of tomorrow, but man, for me, I was at the cinema, watching in disbelief my own flesh and blood going to descend to 200 feet in fog. Part of my mind leaned back, munching popcorn, enjoying the show. Part of it was trying to hem up the localizer, and sweat was running free, between 110 and 140 degrees.

And Glen came in with "You are at the localizer and cleared to land," and I realized that he had done all he could for me, and the moment of truth was at hand.

Hear me. I'm no kamikaze; I had heard them tell the Herky bird that Ellington was 700. I had a Plan Two; a missed approach and a night in some plastic motel in Houston. But I was committed, too. I must see the Bull. At last, now, after all these months of imagined terror, I must call him out. Toro! Toro!

Oh, why 'n hell can't I hold a good localizer course? It's a learned skill, that's why, and I have gotten rusty to its subtle tones. Sinking into grayness, I made it academic. I was back at Bob Marsh Aviation in the simulator. It is all academic. If I don't make it, I can just flick off the switches and get out and face the sneers. Also, I was thinking, this will be sudden and not hurt much. Also thinking, in the next 20 seconds I am going to find out something I need very much to know. And so I descended, splitting my mind between the wandering needles of glide slope, localizer and all that. Reasoning, rationalizing with myself and betting nothing less than life, sweet life.

Do you know that the Earth greens into obscurity when you are near her? A dark, dank greenness of Earth. I was aware of her closeness; playing fortissimo with the rudders. Oh, gentle Cessna, mother of all aircraft, gentle, broad-winged bird, forgive us our trespasses. Earth was nigh. And then the lights. The crucifix of lights. Not all the candles burning yellow in St. Peter's could be more holy than this. "I got the lights." Hell, I could have landed on a postage stamp from there.

What matter 4,000 feet range?

What matter that I could not see across the field in the fog? Stearmans, Cubs, Airknockers, I can land short. And I was still holding Glen's hand. I had asked him not to make me change to tower at the marker for that is the most crucial time, and no time to be playing with the radio. Glen Martinka carried me to the ramp, like a father holding up his newborn son.

I am curious. Even to death, always curious about life and all its processes. I took my pulse. One hundred and sixteen over a normal Southern-boy 72. Not bad; they don't call in the astronauts until the pulse reaches 155. I was well below the screaming point. But the hands shook. The line man laughed, "I don't think you are ready to repair any watches." Right.

"To put your life in danger from time-to-time breeds saneness in dealing with day-to-day trivialities." My personal minimums are still 800 and one mile, but the terror factor is gone.

Chapter 11
Cajuns

Out at the grass airport, we were discussing the perversity of sky divers. Mustache Ken McGill, the pilot of Old Blind Barnabas the Second, the jump plane, pointed to the Cessna 190: "Just look at that thing. Look at where they put the wheels, way out there on the end of those big, long springs. My God! No wonder they prefer to leap out and come home on their own devices."

Old Blind Barnabas the First was lost to us last year when its pilot encountered a secret ditch. All there was to walk away from were the hard iron parts, the big, round engine and those wheels way out there on the ends of long springs.

But McGill says the jump troopers are a special pain. Big, smelly, bare-armed and hairy, they make crude jokes and obscene gestures and put their boots all over the cabin. Worst of all, you have to stay alert for the "last man out" caper. If he can, one of them will lunge for the keys, switch off your engine, and fall out the door waving your keys and mouthing something unintelligible into the slipstream.

It's no problem, of course. You're right over the airport at 10,000 feet, and all you have to do is make one good landing. It's just the humiliation of the thing.

Then A. J. Judice, the crazy Cajun, spoke up on the special problems of skydiving crawfish. Cajun is one of several nicknames given to the Arcadians who were cast out of France and then Canada as a public service several hundred years ago and who overpopulated the low-lying and swampy areas of

Louisiana and Texas. They are noted for their zest for life, love, boudin sausage and crawfish. The less you know about boudin, the better you will like it.

The Cajun culture here is typified by Landry and LeBlanc, Cessna 180 floatplane pilots out of Lafayette. LeBlanc was once standing on a float popping the engine for Landry when the propeller caught in his suspenders, whirled him around five times and cast him up on a shrimp-boat dock a limp heap of rags.

Landry shut the engine down, rushed up to LeBlanc and cried out,
"Speak to me!"

To which LeBlanc replied, "Why should I speak to you? I pass you five times a minute ago and you don't speak to me."

Judice specializes in breeding and racing crawfish. He told us of a recent attempt to import a stud crawfish from Rome. He had the stud and his bride safely but illegally under his beret during the flight to Shannon, Ireland, keeping them alive by pouring Martinis into his beret.

He had a few bad moments with Italian customers before leaving Rome. His beret kept squirming, and the sensation on his scalp was indescribable. Upon arriving in Ireland, he found both crawfish dead. Dead but smiling. He figures that they bred themselves to death. Next time, separate berets.

But about how he gets them to bail out of an airplane: He has a radio-controlled, five-foot-span model of a Stearman. He smears the area around the cockpit with boudin; the crawfish works his way out of the cockpit for a nip, and whisk! The wind snaps the chute open.

His backup system for balked jumps is a timer that slides back a cover on the cockpit floor, revealing a lifelike photograph of a hungry Cajun.

He claims the crawfish always gives a scream and vaults right out.

Unfortunately, the Stearman was lost to us for further verification and photographing. It went out of control during the Diamond Jubilee celebration at Port Arthur, buzzing and awakening the crew of a racing sailboat and then, upon landing on the ceremonial grounds, colliding with a metal keg of tap beer in a brave effort to avoid a crowd of thousands.

Chapter 12
Ghost Squadron

They are all Colonels in the Confederate Air Force, that aging collection of men and of the warplanes that saved the world in the summer of 1942. A loosely knit bunch, made up mostly of professional Texans, they travel over the country with their priceless flying relics like MacNamara's Band, "playing at wakes and weddings and every fancy ball."

They are self-supporting but always broke, passing the Stetson through the crowd "to keep them old birds flyin'." But they are one of the best airshow attractions in the world, swooping down upon the tiny, upturned faces with that chilling sound that once filled the air over Normandy's beaches.

I watched them before the great crowd at Galveston with mixed emotions. Hungry to hear those Allison supercharged V-12s moan their song just once more. Touched by the deep rumble of the distant B-17, that proud queen that killed so many of us so young. Delighted in the folksy way they taxied up and parked them in a row of war paint and let the ropes down so all of us could press forward to touch, to smell, to see. Not the museum's dusted varnish, but the hot mink smell of a twin-row radial engine, still slick in its own slung oil.

Little boys with wonderous eyes were hoisted up on the shoulders of granddads: "... We had a Dilbert lootinant that flew one of these Wildcats into five parked planes. ...sent him home as a Jap ace ... har har ..."

A colonel with gray hair and bourbon-blossom nose was sitting on the wing now in his gray cowboy outfit signing the little boy's autograph book.

Do I wish they would take themselves more seriously? If England could afford a group like this, they would call themselves the Royal Academy for the Preservation of etc., etc., and be wearing club ties and velvet vests. The manners and morals of this group are strictly America, love it or leave it, backyard beer and barbecue. But is this bad? I don't know.

Then the shark-mouthed P-40 zig-zagged smartly into its ramp space, crossing between me and the reddening sun. For an instant, every bold rivet stood highlighted in molten gold. The hawk-faced pilot was a black cutout, the sun behind his Stetson touching the gaunt cheeks. It was like I was seeing all the P-40s at once, in all their flaming battles, and all the men who flew them to glory—seeing them all at one instant.

These men call themselves the Ghost Squadron; they are still 18-year-olds, who have remembrances of things long past with these flying fragments of the mightiest armada that ever swept clean the skies.

But do they have the right to do this? To fly these things instead of letting them sleep safe like sculpture in museums? One by one, they will go in. Fifty-year-old reflexes and high-strung machines built for a few hours in battle, now fatigued with 30 years' age. One by one, they'll stop time forever. Wonderfully. Gloriously.

But should they? I don't know.

I came home, put on my old flying suit, my helmet and goggles—the new ones that fit over the bifocals. I climbed into the cockpit of that 25-year-old PT-13D Stearman and ripped off and wrote "Glory" in the sky. Flew it until the cage of wires sang its song, and thought of what terrible secrets are hidden in those ancient wooden wing spars. Flew it until the prop blast made my head clear and 18 years old again, as it always does. Then I decided:

Those old boys are as crazy as bessie bugs.

Chapter 13
Hawk Lips

"Alan," I said, "let's take the kids and go see what's happening at the airport." We collected little Chris, Eric, Matthew and Gordon IV and ended up in a motherly old Cessna 172. Man, it looked like a barn loft full of owls. When I looked back over my shoulder, I couldn't see anything but big, round eyes everywhere.

"You little punks really want to fly with Grandpa?" I asked.

"Yeah, yeah, let's go! Take off!"

So we went up and bumped around for a while and it got very quiet; they were strapped down so deep they couldn't see out. What difference will it make, I thought, if we have a few kids floating around in the cabin? We unstrapped them and let them stand up. "Now don't play with the door handle. That first step is a long one."

"Hey, just like little model cars down there. Hey, look at that little-bitty train! Gollee, ain't it purty?"

We got to see eight parachutists come out of two jump planes, and we got to see the glider cut loose from the towplane, and we watched all this high color floating and gliding down through the student traffic.

After we landed, I parked the car out near the runway overrun, where they launch and land the glider. It was a wonderful place to park the kids, who were pretending they were sky divers and were practicing bailing out of the Buick. They put on sunglasses and undid the shoulder harnesses and shouted commands. Periodically, all four of them would fly out the windows.

It got to be my turn to fly the glider, and Alan made all the kids come over and kiss Grandpa good-bye and get a last look at the old man. The towplane hauled me up to 2,000 feet and I cut loose.

I had noticed this hawk circling over our corner of the field. A hawk is always hunting a thermal, especially a thermal that might be over mice, and I think he figured the grandkids were mice and was planning on carrying one off with him. Anyway, I shouldered into the thermal with the hawk and circled at about 40 mph in zero sink. He had his wings spread all the way out, glorious and free, and his pinions out on the ends were trembling, like the glider's wing tips. He was right out there, looking me over like he had pulled up alongside and was going to write me a ticket.

Well, the hawk and I started to play. He could turn faster than I could, but I could ease in on him. It was so beautiful to look out there and see that big bird so close. If I got too near, he would duck under and come up on the other side. I dropped the nose a little and picked up speed, and began to whistle at about 60—which, for a glider, is moving along—and I looked up there and the hawk was still with me. He had sort of hunched up his wings, and the slipstream was just tearing at his feathers. He looked at me with hooded eyes, and that hawk had a savage little grin on his mouth, the wind blowing his lips back over his teeth, and his eyes sparkling. I could see glints of red and gold as he flashed in the sun. I swear he was enjoying himself.

Then it dawned on me that we were gliding farther and farther from the airport. I remembered a story about a sailplane pilot on the West Coast who had followed a seagull, riding a wave of lift, and when they got way out to sea, the gull sort of laughed, turned around toward land and started flapping his wings. Ain't no way you can flap your wings in a glider. So I let the hawk win our game and eased on back to the landing slot.

I was a little low, and I'm sorry about getting bark on the wing of the glider, but they ought to do something about that tree at the end of the runway. Actually, it's more like a bush.

We were driving back to the hangar when I got to thinking what it would sound like if a transient pilot who had never seen the grass airport before were to call in, "Ahhh, this is Piper 34Xray, give me your airport advisory."

I can hear our line man come on and say, "Well, we got three students in the pattern on touch and go, we have two jump planes at 10,000 feet, there are eight jumpers free-falling, a glider has just been released at 2,000 feet over the active runway, radio-controlled models are aloft over the ramp, six Japanese kites at 1,500 on the downwind leg. We have a hawk on a short final for a mouse, a '73 Buck on the active with four kids just bailing out of it, the active runway is 12 and look out for the tree. Actually, it's more of a small bush."

The guy would think he had called up the zoo, and he'd go off and land somewhere else and have his radio worked on. It was a beautiful day at the little grass airport.

As long as I live, I'll remember looking out at that hawk right beside me, feathers rippling, tears streaming out of his eyes and a big grin on his face. That's kind of hard for a hawk to do, because a hawk has real stiff lips.

Chapter 14
Night Hawk

The night was hushed, soft as velvet. One tall window in the old airport building was yellow-lighted. The rotating beacon on top swept its light across sleeping airplanes on the flight line; metal glinted cold.

By flashlight and by touch I crept around the friendly old bird, and then sat awhile in the dark cabin, in the musty aluminum-tobacco-gasoline smells, reaching out.

I remembered the story about the student who carried a flashlight with a magnetized base and carefully laid it on the cowl beside the compass, and for the rest of that night all he could find with his compass was his flashlight.

I remembered my first night flight. My instructor and I got lost. We flew toward Lufkin, which is about north, and the lights of Lufkin grew and grew until they filled the horizon and became Houston, which is about east. Nonetheless, we seemed closer in the dark cockpit than two men do in the daylight, and his voice carried clear as he passed along the hard-earned lessons of pilot lore. About the hidden night clouds, and how one light on the ground will betray you into vertigo, and to "curve in a little on final, and carry a little power till you're in."

The first time alone when the edge of night came forbidding, like flying into wrongness. Dusk deepening on the earth below while I was still aloft in distant, lonely light. And of how cities hundreds of miles apart glowed upon the horizon, and how easy it was to find other planes. Delta cleared down to six was that winking red beacon descending, and Braniff reporting on frequency was that distant star. Once, in a bunch of them, I said, "and that's me, the low and slow one." And a big voice chuckled softly and said, "Gotcha." Even the voices are softer on a clear night.

Our grass airport is black as the pits of hell. Coming home when the beacon is out, you steer for the only place in town where there are no lights at all and tell yourself clearly that you do know how to let yourself down into there.

You know because you have practiced. Practiced going to coal-black on takeoff, practiced landing with the light until you are good enough to pretend the landing light has failed, then practiced with it switched off, feeling all your flying senses prickle alive as you settle dark between those pale runway eyes.

And practicing tonight yes—and for the love of it, too. Taxiing slow, watching nested night hawks start up and swerve away on bladed wings. On takeoff, the old Cessna is enveloped in lift at once; the wings feel as though they grow out from my shoulders. The night air is full of lift.

I am a tiny green light and a red light droning softly over my sleeping city. Even the junkyards are lovely. It's all so peaceful and orderly from here, like God had stayed over from Easter morning and got it all together for once. The wings are so fat with lift, there is no sense of motion. I may park it here and climb out and stroll up and down on that broad wing and have a good cigar and contemplate the ancient stars.

Chapter 15
Cross City

I called aviation weather from Central Brevard and they said, "It's good out of here, but there's a front with thunderstorm activity at ..." Guess where. Cross City. If there's ever going to be bad weather in Florida, it's gonna be at Cross City. That's what the line boy told us when we came in. Never forget anything a line boy says.

The sun was shining, the sky was high and clear, wings bent back. It was gorgeous. We were smoking good tobacco, leaning back in the seats. Roney, the Navy guy, was already asleep all over the back seat. We knew it couldn't last.

We passed Cross City and came into what you might call a declining sky. It looked like a tunnel that had caved in. Now, there is a little hook in the Florida coastline here, formed by Apalachee Bay. Out on the point of this bay is the town of Apalachicola, and the only place up in the middle of this empty coastal curve is the Saint Teresa Light & Mud Flats. It's a little Catholic lighthouse and mud flat, and there's not a thing out there—not even Saint Teresa, who checked out a long time ago.

By the time we got to Saint Teresa, we were in light rain. Let's say heavy rain. We looked up ahead and there was nothing but water. The curving coastline had disappeared. The Gulf of Mexico was standing on edge. Vertical.

I had been listening to all those depressing weather reports from all over the Florida panhandle. Tallahassee was saying, "Ceiling, three inches.

Visibility, nine millimeters. Fog. Bubonic plague. Do not land here for six months."

Alan cried out, "Hey, there's an airport!" Trying to dump speed and altitude at the same time, I made a tight 180 at about 100 feet, thanking the old Stearman for all it had taught me and turning slightly gray at the temples.

The G load woke up our hero, returning from Danang, who was sleeping it off on the back seat. He fell into the window. He opened his eyes, expecting to see the sky, and was looking down into a pine tree.

I said, "Alan, we are going to have a look at that little airstrip." The only difference between it and the rest of the swamp was that it had a windsock.

He was looking from his side on the pass. "It's very wet. I think it has fish." We flew on.

"Alan," I said, in a very casual, offhand manner, "we will try that highway to the lighthouse, but I can't seem to find it now."

"You went right over it."

"Why didn't you say something?"

"I didn't want to disturb you. Anyway, you couldn't have got into it with a torpedo."

We were flying back now, only there was no back to go. Tallahassee was saying, "Cross City, ceiling three feet. Visibility nothing. Heavy rain and high grass."

We continued back-tracking the coastline in our little slice of wet, gray sky. I decided to consult Tallahassee. The man in the safe cement tower said, "What is your exact position?

I told him I was down on the coastline by Saint Teresa and that I was about snookered.

He said, "Call Tyndall Field."

Tyndall yawned and stretched and threw aside his comic book and said, "Fly arrgh rowr-rr, raarrh niner nar nar-r ..." fade, fade, last we heard of Tyndall. Probably vectored some pelican in and left us out there on the Saint Teresa mud flats.

Speaking close to the windshield, I said, "Let us avoid any hasty decisions of gloom and look upon the brighter side of this matter. We are not lost. We have plenty of gas. We are just a little low on sky. We will proceed in an orderly, cautious fashion back in the direction of Cross City, a sound decision based on there being no other choice."

I noticed that the omni was beginning to respond to strong urgings from Cross City. A beautiful airport, abandoned, I think, the concrete checkered in rich grass. The landing was not too bad for a pilot in such a high state of thankfulness.

A little old man came out of a small hut, the only building in sight. I asked, "Is this a public building?"

The little old man said, "The door is 40 inches wide. If you cannot get through it, it is no fault of mine." I knew we had a contest going.

"Where can we get the weather?"

"This is a United States Weather Bureau facility."

"Well, what's the weather?"

"I don't know. I don't give out the weather. I just record it on these instruments, for which I am paid to do by the Government."

I walked in and all around. There was a ton of weather equipment humming to itself, but no readout. "But how can we get the weather?" I asked the elf of the machines.

"Well," he said with a cackle, "you could get in your airplane and spiral up and call Tallahassee, except that the weather is too bad for that. Tee hee hee."

Chapter 16
Graduation Day

I have graduated, I have grown antlers, I have soloed a 450 Bull Stearman at last! After all those good years flying Mitchell's two holer—that lovely, muley 220 Stearman—flying it until we wore out the 220 and replaced it with a Lycoming 300. That made it hornier but did not unlock the secrets of what happens when you line up one of those stubby, big-engined blind bats on the strip and open the throttle on 450 horses. But most of the 450s are working airplanes, single-seaters, and there are some manners to consider before asking a man to let you go out and play with a $20,000 ag plane just to see if you can hack it.

Then there appeared a brand-new 450 two-holer, the Bull Stearman, built in a Winnie, Texas, bowling alley by Jeff Jenkins and Ronnie Langlois—Jeff who was begat of Mitchell, Ronnie who was begat of Spartan and Glen Parker (who was the begetter of us all). Winnie is a wide spot in the Gulf Coast rice fields, a place of 2,500 souls and six airports and three ag operations, where these two young men have built a dozen immaculate ag Stearmans, and where American Dusters sends students to graduate.

The 450 two-holer is for graduation day the Homecoming Queen.

Ronnie said, "She's a cherry, the last of Glen Parker's new ones. She was still in the cosmoline. We built our jig from her frame." Ronnie and Jeff say they'll never run out of Stearmans. "We got 10 more hid out in barns, and all the jigs and dies and fixtures.

With a load of pipe and a handful of welding rod, we can build them from scratch."

She stood there in the grass and the sun at the end of a double row of single-seat sisters. Chrome yellow, white side panels, looking short-coupled and deep-chested like they do when they put in the 450 P&W and set it well back to keep the balance. Sun danced off the wires and chromed engine parts. That engine, its naked roundness standing out beyond the lines of the fuselage: It was scaring me to death just looking up at it.

In the cockpit, wood-grained panels, new leather-laced coamings, polished wooden stick and even a "self-commencer," as the Cajuns say–a starter. Down the lines of planes, pilots were climbing into cockpits, engines starting, wings rocking, cocky, brave, blatting away. Cherish this: Few men yet look down a row of biplanes from the cockpit.

Jeff was telling me the power settings. The blown P&W will rave up to 38 inches and nearly 3,000 rpm on takeoff, but you only need 27 inches and 1,900 for fast cruise. I was writing it on the back of my hand.

"Let me give you a piece of paper."

"No, man, I want it where I can find it." I asked Jeff what to expect, what to use over the fence. He just grinned. "She'll tell you. You'll really be surprised." That's what I was afraid of.

The starter whined, the big, flat Hamilton windmilled, caught, chopped smoke and the engine settled down, going "bloopa, bloopa, ker-bloopa" deep in her throat, rocking the biplane on her tires. I touched the throttle like it was a serpent, taxied the thing like it was made of blown glass.

The mystery of takeoff had always been how much swerve to expect. The surprise was the unbelievable roar and force of the prop blast. My Bell was trying to fly my head off my neck, I was wishing I had the seat a notch lower, and we were long gone, a pursuit ship, climbing on solid power, wings angled up where other planes stall.

Level now, a feeling of tearing along, airspeed reading 125, the big P&W rumbling, loafing. She sailed up in wingovers like a kite, begging to barrel roll. She nibbled at stalls, burbled, then said "oh, well" and sunk flat. Power-on stalls were pointless, prop-hanging being such an awkward feeling. Jeff tapped his helmet, took it, slowed down and gently snap rolled. Gently. Right around that big engine. But there was no use postponing the moment of truth. Sooner or later, I was going to have to try to land all this.

I arced around for the grass, slipping to find it, to see past Jeff and all those wings and wires and engine parts, feeling her, never looking at the panel. She told me what she needed. We slipped over the fence, lined up true, and she came to nest like a warm dove in the hand. I couldn't believe it. Two more and Jeff made the four-oh sign with his hand and I stopped and let him out. "She's yours. Go up and use her."

Alone, my heart was a song. We climbed up to where it was cold. The sun was low and red, bathing the cockpit, glinting off the windshields and wires. Earth and sky tumbled, we sang, we roared, we made music and love until we were drunk with it all.

Then we chain-looped down and sighed in over the grass and met our long shadow. I parked her in the row with her sisters, hating to turn off the sound of that great-hearted horse of an engine. The 450 is for the Stearman made. I just sat there. A pilot came by and grinned at me, knowing. I reached out my arms, hugging and patting the round of her fuselage. He laughed.

In the pilots' room with coffee and the strong, lean faces, I felt I had graduated. I was one of them. And now I want to share it with you.

I hope you can come out of your flying Chevrolets someday and know all of this, for this is not business, not transportation, or towers or concrete or numbers.

This, dear hearts, is flying.

Chapter 17
Find Your Boy Self Again

What happens after you have flown all the airplanes, made all the money, fought the good fight, and suddenly the golden Septembers are rushing past your wings? Can you ever go back and find your boyish self again? Of simple times and sunny fields when laughter came easily?

C. C. Holt and Dick Taylor did. They went back to Lilienthal—to gliders and the beginnings of flight. They became the patrons of soaring at Houston.

Clover Field lies just south of Houston's sprawl—soon, but not yet, to be choked to death by smog and suburbia. It is an airport of miscellaneous turf runways, as though each previous tenant had beaten a takeoff path in his own favorite direction. The clover is shared with some grazing horses, a snorting circuit of minibikes, a Smith biplane, a Luscombe, some Ercoupes, a Piper Clipper, an abandoned Convair airliner and a black-and-white nanny goat. You can use the goat as a windsock; she feeds upwind. Land upgoat.

The gliders lie tipped in the center of the field in a cluster of automobiles. Lush Marsha, the F-102 jock's wife, will schedule you for a ride or offer a jam sandwich. It is a quiet gathering. They lie upon the grass or rap to Moody Blues coming from the tape deck of the MG, and they gaze upon the Schweizers and Blanik phantoms circling in the blue haze. The sailplanes come droop-snooting in over the oil-rig tower, spoilers tweaking, and stop like blade-winged footballs on the tee, balancing.

The neat little Japanese doctor is getting his rating this weekend. The Korean and the tall Chinese are his friends. The leathery old former B-17 pilot in the scuffed Wellingtons didn't tell anybody he was high-time; he let his touch tell the story and soloed quickly and talked off tall, looking like he had found it at last. The full-blown blonde left her husband and baby at the car and bought a wring-out ride in the Blanik and climbed out after the loops and spins all damp. She led her husband off by the hand with a peculiar glint in her eye. Glider freaks all.

When I sat down in the gaunt-framed Schweizer 2-33 and they closed, I'd never felt more like I belonged. Good vibes flowed between us. Thinking back now, I never missed the engine, except that my left hand had nothing to do. One engine is reason enough for anxiety; two engines make me wary as a cat. No engine seemed as it should be.

Being snatched aloft by the sweaty little Super Cub is a necessary humiliation. The pitch-up, the wild veering and scuffling of being dragged like a box lasts only a moment. Then there is life. Superior life, and one must hold low until the Cub finishes its duty business on the ground and gets airborne itself.

Towing was the most demanding. George Metts's voice came from the rear bassinet: "Just center Jim's rudder on his bald spot and you're in perfect tow."

><

Of all of aviation's needle-and-ball-chasing games, this one is the most diabolical. There is a control lag in the movement of such a long span; it's like straddling a seesaw at the pivot point and trying to keep the board level in shifting winds. There is a bright orange bit of yarn blowing back a tube. It tells you how years of gentle Cessnas and docile Pipers have withered away your rudder feet. I was stirring the stick like mixing a thick chocolate cake when Metts muttered, "It would be better with about half as much of that."

At 2,000 feet, the last sound is the bang of release, and the nylon snarls off after the Cub. After that, you can faintly hear sounds drifting up from earthlings. Ah, then it becomes all that flight was ever supposed to be. Wings sprouted from my shoulders. I wheeled with the silent hawks. The up wing raced against the sky, the down wing seemed to run backward. A bubble of lift and I was stealing from God, wanting to laugh, to sing. After three and solo, I would have to slap my mind and say, "Remember, man, this thing also descendeth, and you will be, you *must* be, perfect in the slot lest you hang among the pears in yonder orchard."

The Schweizer would whisper and strum and make little soft, fluttery sounds, and I lay with my head against her canopy, caught in the trance. But the check ride untranced me. Now that Dick Taylor was in his mean-man FAA suit, I soared too high on tow and got above the Cub and lost him. The rule is release. I asked him if he wanted to see the rest of it. "No."

A miserable wait on the ground, avoiding eyes. I always bust check rides. Then a second chance, and now a precious word on my sparsely printed ticket: glider.

><

Have you ever, in dreams, flown free? It was like that.

Chapter 18
How Safe Is This Thing?

Newspapers love a good, clean airplane-crash story. Let one of your locals be carried away on silvered wings and they move all the rape and robbery stories to inside pages. An airplane accident is front-page.

Let a local pilot deftly land his ailing aircraft on a farm road or field, and before he can walk away unscathed, he has drawn a crowd of reporters. There he is, grinning on the front page, telling of his miraculous escape from the jaws of death. How embarrassing.

All this is most unfortunate, for it perpetuates the old legend that flying is a dangerous and derring-do affair. As a veteran reporter, I should point out to you some obvious logic. "News" is still the telling of the unusual. "Man Bites Dog" is what sells papers.

Airplane wrecks are still "news." On a holiday weekend a dozen of your fellow humans might die in car wrecks and each will get only hometown regrets. But if one dies in a plane crash the story is still spectacular enough to go statewide. Aviation accidents are uncommon enough to still be "news," but their high visibility might worry your family and even yourself as you consider learning to fly.

Aviators love to tell you that the most hazardous part of the trip is behind you as soon as you get out of your car. No so. But according to National Transportation Board statistics, boating is more dangerous than flying little airplanes. Still, buying a ticket and flying on a scheduled airliner is safer than flying one yourself. Staying home in bed is even safer than that.

Most general aviation mishaps are traced to an error in judgment or poor flying technique. And this is most often such a simple thing as running out of gas or flying into bad weather. So set yourself this early goal of planning to learn all the common-sense techniques and judgmental values that you can.

I hope this does not discourage you, but a Navy study revealed that a person's driving record tends to reflect what kind of a pilot he is going to be.

On the question of the mechanical condition of the airplane, automobiles should have it so good. By federal law, your training plane gets an annual inspection of every hinge, cable, fitting, engine part, and accessory it's got. The airplane is pretty well taken apart and brought up to factory specs for its annual. And all airplanes for hire–that is, for commercial use such as training–also get a one-hundred-hour inspection. This is similar to the annual but involves only the most common and everyday inspection and preventive work. Also, any well-maintained airplane gets an oil change at 25 hours; the mechanic usually checks the spark plugs, too.

All these inspections and maintenance items, except for the most simple, are performed by an aviation mechanic whose license was harder for him to get than the one you are going for now. And there are two log books that stay in the airplane: *airframe* and engine. The mechanic logs a description of the work done in these permanent and official documents, and signs it off with his own precious name and certificate number. Wouldn't you love to see auto mechanics doing that?

Good maintenance is a serious and everyday part of aviation.

><

Now, as to the first doubting question: How stoutly is this thing made? A factory-built airplane is the nearest thing you will ever find to something that technically came down an assembly line but is actually hand-crafted. If one of the rivets that holds the aluminum sin of an airplane together is canted, dimpled in too deep, or improperly flared, gets found, circled with a wax pencil, drilled out, and done over. The amount of handwork and piecework that goes into an airplane is one of the reasons they cost so much.

Before an airplane goes into production, the prototype must be flown through certification test flights by engineering test pilots. After an airplane is certified, each and every one is taken out and flown by a production test pilot to make sure this individual airplane does exactly what it is certified to do.

Every single part in the airplane—rivets, nuts, bolts, all of it—must be certified before it can be built into the plane. This certification process can take years. Done by the maker himself but to FAA standards, the tedious certification process is one of the reasons for the reluctance of the makers to change anything. That, and the characteristic conservatism of the aircraft manufacturing industry.

And these light, flimsy-looking, stamped-out airplanes are surprisingly strong. Part of the certification of a training plane is that its wings must be able to bear four times its normal weight. That means that an average 2,000-pound training plane has wings that will bear an 8,000-pound load. And that's just the test before anything bends. There is strength beyond that.

One happy result of all this care and caring is that, unlike automobiles, airplanes last forever. Barring damage, or corrosion, an old airplane that is well cared for just gets older and worth more money. Many of the wartime DC-3s are still in daily commercial service. My own 1968 Mooney Ranger is not unusual in being worth now about twice what I paid for it.

The one ray of sunshine in the clouds of rising costs of flying is that a good airplane is a good investment.

Unlike auto engines, which just run until they quit or until the body rots off from around then, aircraft engines have a manufacturer's recommended span of useful life. Engine life is measured in terms of hours of use, and the TBO (time before overhaul) of a good light-plane power plant is between 1,200 and 2,000 hours. Average use of a private plane is surprisingly low: 200 hours per year, although training planes in use every day roll up their hours much faster than that.

When an engine reaches TBO, the private owner groans and forks up a few thousand for an engine exchange or for having his present engine rebuilt to factory-new specs. The big flight schools usually replace their fleet at about half TBO. You can read the hours of the engine of any plane by looking at the total on the Hobbs meter, or on the tachometer.

><

Once, when I was flying the old Stearman biplane which belongs to George Mitchell M&M Air Service (a large ag flying outfit in Beaumont, Texas), I went in and told his chief pilot, Earl West, that the old radial engine sure was running smooth. West grinned at me with the other face of flying and said,

"When they get smooth like that they're fixing to swarm you."

Actually, airplane engines are quite simple and seldom experience catastrophic failure. Airplanes have limped back and landed with such awful-sounding things as blown cylinder heads, broken crankshafts, stuck valves, burned pistons. An airplane engine nearly always warns the pilot that something is going wrong by a power failure. It slows down and, as we say, begins *running rough.*

Within a few short hours you will get so accustomed to how a healthy airplane engine sounds that any change in its tone will activate long-unused ear muscles and cause your ears to get pointy and stand right up. One of the bits of other-face humor in flying is that when you're crossing hostile terrain such as forests, lakes, or rocks in a single-engine plane, the engine sooner or later goes into "auto rough," or "over-water rough." This is a pilot-induced symptom caused by an overactive imagination in a situation where there is no good landing place available.

>﹤

In all my happy years of flying, I have never had an engine just pack up on me and quit cold in a situation where I could not get the ailing airplane back down onto a runway. Of course, knowing where the nearest runway is at all times is a great help in bringing a getting-sick airplane back home again. Part of your training syllabus will be how to recognize and cope with in-flight emergencies and other "what if" situations.

The entire structure of student flying is oriented around safety. "To safely perform ..." is the most often repeated qualification in the Federal Air Regulations under the subtitle "Aeronautical Skill." Statistically, the record of private flying improves slightly each year. But there's always the vague but meaningful "faulty pilot technique." This dark tent loosely covers most of the "he just shoulda known-betters."

Running into instrument weather, running out of gas, and running out of airspeed still add up to over half the accident causes.

Crashes, for the most part, are perfectly good-running airplanes being driven into the ground by someone who decided the rules didn't apply to him.

As you stand at the threshold of flying and wonder how safe it is, remember that the primary accident cause is squirming right there inside your own skull. Only you can control that.

Chapter 19
Who me, fly this thing?

In all the good romance stories about flying, the pilot awakens first, now ignoring her smooth shoulders, and goes and stands in the doorway gazing at the sky. He sniffs the air for rain, notes and remembers the direction and force of the wind, casts a wary eye upon the height and movement of the clouds. Weather–that never tiring adversary he must soon come to solitary grips with.

This scene is not so easy to carry off with style if you live in an apartment and the door opens out to the elevators. But watch your flight instructor as you and he step out of the operations building and onto the *flight line*. If he does not cast a habitual and judgmental eye upon the sky, then either he has not been flying very long or he's been reading the wrong books.

If the *ceiling* is too low, or the winds too strong, he will tell you to come back another day.

Let your cheerful acceptance of non-flying weather be the first rule that will guide you evermore. Flying is not intrinsically dangerous, but too many good-running airplanes are driven into the ground by pilots who choose to continue on into adverse weather.

A definition of "adverse weather" must be qualified by the experience of the pilot and the equipment in his aircraft. At one end of the scale is the low-time student or *private pilot*, flying a small airplane which is equipped with only the most basic *flight instruments*. At the other extreme is the experienced three-man crew of a jet airliner which is fitted out with the most advanced *blind-flying* instruments, on-board radar, and *de-icing* devices. Adverse weather has a widely different meaning to these two widely different segments of aviation, and to every level of experience and equipment in between. The basic line of demarcation, the one you will hear spoke the most, is *VFR* weather and *IFR* weather.

- VFR means *Visual Flight Rules*, a descriptive term that means the pilot will be able to see out the window and fly by visual reference to the ground.
- IFR means *Instrument Flight Rules,* which describes a plane and crew that can fly in clouds with no visual reference to the ground but instead can maintain controlled flight and navigate precisely by reference to instruments only.
- VFR means there must be three miles visibility at the airport and the overcast, or cloud base level, must be at least 1,000 feet above ground. Away from the controlled airspace of an airport, VFR is a more relaxed one-mile visibility and "clear of clouds."

The study of weather and the lifelong accumulation of weather judgment will be one of the most interesting and important parts of your entry into aviation.

><

So weather permitting, you and your pilot will walk out onto the flight line toward the *training plane*. Since the early 1930s, when the first good ones were developed, training planes are small, simple and sturdy of design, and easy and fun to fly. Without any stigma, like the training wheels on a bike, or training pants on a kid, training planes are often owned and flown just for the joy of it by pilots who earn their living flying airliners.

Your instructor will tell you what kind of a trainer this one is, and he will start the demonstration flight by describing what he is doing in the little *pre-flight* ceremony that we call the *walk-around* inspection.

Even the lofty airline captains send the *co-pilot* out in the cold to do this menial and repetitive chore. If, in your coming flying years, you ever see a pilot do what we contemptuously call "kick the tires and light the fires," you can discount him as a careless, foolish person.

This routine pre-flight inspection is important because there is just no easy way you can pull off the side of the road and look under the hood once you have launched in an airplane.

Your pilot will do the walk-around in a manner detailed for him in the owner's manual. Unlike the "owner's manual" which comes with a new car (really just a sales brochure), the aircraft owner's manual is full of engineering facts, data, operations charts, and performance tables. Its contents are the findings of the engineering test pilots, gathered up during the design, testing, and certification of that airplane. As each plane comes off the assembly line, a production test pilot flies it to make sure it will do what the book says it will do. The owner's manual is a *Federal Aviation Authority* (FAA) approved document, a carefully written work intended to serve you, and sometimes brought into courtrooms as evidence during accident litigation.

The book stays with the airplane, but a good FBO will have low-cost copies of it available to you. Buy one and spend a night with it before you spend too many days with the airplane.

If he is serious, the instructor will invite you to sit in the left seat. Traditionally, the throne of the *pilot in command,* but in *dual instruction,* the teacher rides right seat. Let him tell you how to close the door. Different planes latch in different ways.

Watch as he goes down his *check list.* All well managed airplanes have a printed check list handy as a reminder of engine start-up and all the other procedures before takeoff. There is another section of it for pre-landing and shutdown. Pilots do not use a check list because they are incapable of remembering these basics; they use it to reinforce their memory. If you ever make a takeoff with the uneasy feeling that you have forgotten something, you probably have. And you probably did not use your check list that time.

Light aircraft have a simple key-turn starter, but unlike autos, they are never "out of gear" when the engine is running. First, your instructor will set the brakes, which are activated by toe pressure on top of the *rudder pedals* in modern trainers. The engine bangs smartly to life but seems to be running rough and full of vibrations as compared to an idling car. Part of that is the natural vibrations of the small, four-cylinder, air-cooled power plants that all trainers have, and part of it comes from the propeller biting the air: the *prop blast,* blowing back along the fuselage, and strumming its tail surfaces. All of this smoothes out and takes on a very reassuring blend of touch and sound once the airplane gets into the element it is designed for: the air.

><

Airplanes waddle ungracefully and slowly across the ground. What we have here is a tricycle about 30 feet wide being steered by its *nose wheel.* The *rudder* and nose wheel are linked together in most trainers to facilitate ground steering, but sharp turns are made by holding one brake. Aircraft brakes operate independently of each other with enough holding power in the braking system to maneuver out of tight parking places on the *ramp* by locking the brake on one *main wheel* and pivoting the airplane right around it.

Sometimes on the demonstration ride your instructor will let you taxi the airplane out, telling you how to get used to this odd manner of ground steering with your feet.

Watch how your instructor's head swivels, always looking from side to side as you taxi out. Same thing later in flight. He's not nervous or restless, he's careful. Aircraft operate in a see-and-be-seen environment. The silk scarf at the neck of World War I fighter pilots was not altogether a romantic affectation. Tucked into the top of the heavy leather flying coat, the scarf held body heat in and served as a smooth neck bearing for those pilots in open cockpits who stayed alive by searching the skies.

We are indoors in a heated cabin now, and Richthofen's Fokker is not about to pounce on us, but pilot neck-swiveling goes on just the same. A midair collision can spoil your whole day.

You will be flying out of one of two kinds of airports. The larger, busier ones are *controlled airports,* characterized by a control tower, within which an *Air Traffic Controller* (ATC) directs the flow of traffic by two-way radio. The busiest of these also use radar to visual and manage the flow of aircraft. At a controlled airport, the pilot will be on the radio before he ever moves the plane, and still on it through various changing frequencies until it's finally parked again.

In the order of their usage, the most common radio frequencies from a controlled airport are:

1. *Ground control*: visual direction from the tower to aircraft and vehicles moving on the ground.

2. *Tower:* visual control from the tower of aircraft landing or taking off.

3. *Approach control:* two-way radio or radar control of traffic approaching or departing from the airport, usually within a radius of about 15 to 20 miles of the airport.

4. *En route control:* the separation of aircraft on cross-country flights, mostly done by radar today. Also called *center,* enroute controllers give traffic and sometimes weather advisories to both IFR and VFR traffic.

5. *Flight service stations* (FSS): Not usually involved in traffic controlling, but on call to all pilots for detailed weather updating and for the airborne filing or amending of *flight plans.*

Aeronautical charts show an Airport Traffic Area around each airport that has an operating control tower. This is a five-mile circle, extending upward to 3,000 feet above ground level (AGL).

Control Zones, or *Terminal Control Areas* (TCA) are larger areas of airport control with shapes that vary to meet the needs of the locale.

Your first impression may be that flying is mostly aeronautical chart reading, radio talking, and frequency changing. You are partly right, but don't let this put you off. In aviation, as in driving, things get more tranquil as you get farther out into the countryside. Student training is done in a designated remote *practice area* where they leave you pretty much alone.

If you begin flying from a smaller rural airport you will find no control tower, no *controlled airspace,* no radio. Many small fields have a

UNICOM frequency that pilots share in a kind of a "Hey, Joe" atmosphere.

At both controlled and non-controlled airports, your pilot will stop before he moves out onto the active runway and perform his last-minute rituals of the *run-up*: checking the engine under the increased power, reading the instruments, moving the controls to see that they are free. When he is through with this last part of the check list, and satisfied that the airplane is ready for flight, he will tell the tower: "Two-seven November, ready at three zero."

The first part of that is his radio call sign taken from the last three digits of the registration number of the plane, and the second part is the number of the active runway.

Runways are numbered according to their *magnetic compass* heading, minus the last digit. An airplane lined up on runway three zero will have a compass reading of 300. The other end of the runway would bear the *reciprocal heading* of 120 degrees and go by the family name of runway one two. Runway numbers are painted at the *threshold* of each runway in numbers as big as will fit.

Once the tower has said, "Cleared for takeoff," your pilot will probably take one last look up the *approach* end of the runway to see for himself that no inbound aircraft are about to land, and take a look down the runway to be sure it is all clear.

At a non-controlled airport, he will most surely do this because the traffic is self-directed, but even with the tower's OK to go the pilot will still look. No matter what tower or anyone else tells him, he is *pilot in command.* Like a ship captain at sea, and for exactly the same reason, the pilot in command has total authority because he is also totally responsible.

The pilot can override ground controllers. "Not able" can be sufficient reply. But when he returns to earth, and the FAA sends for him as his mother once did, he'd better have a good solid reason for that "not able."

For as long as your instructor flies beside you he is pilot in command, but once alone, even as a student, you will be the *PIC.*

With the airplane lined up along the centerline of the runway, the pilot now slowly opens the *throttle.* The airplane is going to make the most noise it ever makes during this full-power takeoff.

There is no neck-snapping acceleration, just a steady, powerful gaining of speed. When the plane reaches the *flying speed,* your pilot will gently ease back the *control wheel,* or *yoke* as it's just as often called, and the airplane will lift off and begin a gentle climb.

><

This instant, this first sensation of flight as the ground drops away below, is one of those enchanted moments that has hooked so many of us into flying. There is the rush, the feeling of the wings growing fat with *lift,* the plane responsive and eager to fly.

There have been times like these when I have felt that the wings sprouted right out of my shoulders. Takeoff is a moment of elation.

Your pilot will reduce the throttle setting from 100 percent takeoff power to the still-strong climb power shortly after takeoff. At a controlled airport he will receive *vectors,* directions to turn and fly in, and continue to climb. The nose of the plane is slightly above the horizon in a climb, and in a turn the earth seems to turn.

At cruising altitude–3,000 or 4,000 feet for demo rides or instructional flights–the pilot will reduce power again, bringing the nose level with the horizon, and the engine will quiet down. In level flight, today's trainers will cruise at a little over 100 miles per hour, but there is no sensation of speed. That's because there is nothing to compare your speed to. You are aloft, distant, as if suspended, and there's no onrushing traffic or blurred telephone poles whipping by. At first, only reading the airspeed indicator will give you any idea of how fast you are flying. Later you will be able to sense the speed by many subtle things–the sound of the slip-stream, the feet of the controls.

Your first view of the world from a cockpit of a small plane is sort of like meeting a woman for the first time with only her facial expressions to guide you. Later you will know more of where you are with her, even if you can't see her face–by the way her heels hit the floor, by the way she sets her coffee cup down.

Your pilot may invite you to have a go at flying the plane yourself. As with the lady, don't grab or do anything too suddenly.

The pilot probably has been holding the yoke by his finger tips. You do the same. Later you'll find yourself grabbing fistfuls of it. If you ever look down at your hands and see white knuckles, it's time to turn loose a minute, take a few deep breaths, flex your fingers some. Airplanes are to be held like scrolls, not hammers.

Your pilot may show you how to do some gentle banking turns and climbs. You'll find the control motions are almost natural. He should show you the designed stability built into modern trainers: hands off, they tend to seek straight and level flight by themselves.

You probably won't have the feeling of teetering height that one gets when peering down from a tall building. The cabin of the plane seems to be an intact solid and reassuring little world of its own. And if this is a good demo flight you won't come away from it overwhelmed at the idea that you have committed yourself to learning to manage this small island in the sky all by yourself.

Aside from the beauty of it, the sense of grace and motion, the view, the feeling of freedom and of having exercised some new power and control over your own hitherto ground-bound existence, flying can be a very bumpy ride. Doesn't seem like it should be, planing through nothing but air like that, but the air can be rough at times.

There are no such things as "air pockets." That is a misnomer left over from the early and unknowing days of flight. There are downdrafts and updrafts, but the nearest you will ever come to an air pocket will be the air left in your pockets after you have paid for the experience of flight.

But if your first ride is on a hot summer mid-afternoon, the plane will slam, bang, thud, rise, fall in a constant restless manner, as it travels through this smooth and empty-looking air. This light turbulence is caused by unevenly heated columns of air rising from the ground. Called *convection currents,* they bob and joggle your wings. No mystery here. Plowed ground, sand, rock, and barren soil tend to reflect more rising heat than water, vegetation and forests.

Above the usual low level of scattered summer clouds, the air is cooler and deliciously smooth and undisturbed as it is in the early-morning, late-afternoon, and night flight. Something to know if you are troubled with motion sickness at first.

Popping a motion-sickness pill is OK if you are only going as a passenger, but any over-the-counter or prescription drug that induces drowsiness, as these often do, is something that even the boldest of us eagles avoid as pilots.

><

Persistent airsickness really did discourage and embarrass me at first. For a while I brought a small bucket and flew with it between my knees. Once I actually began to pilot the plane, I was never troubled again. But I can still get "mal-de-air" riding as a passenger, especially in the back seat. I can find relief by tipping my head back as far as it will go; I try for horizontal, close my eyes, and put my mind far away. Once on the ground, a cold 7-Up is the best stomach settler for me. And finally, airsickness ain't funny, although you may be the only person who believes this at the time. There is also a really mean old aviation tradition about who cleans up the airplane.

Wishing you a happy belly on your demo ride, let's head for "home plate," as the Navy calls it. Don't feel embarrassed if you feel turned around even over your own home town and can't find the direction back to the airport. That happened to all of us, too. The scratchings of man not only form fascinating patterns on the face of this earth, but they do look different from the air. And I have yet to get tired of the experience of just flying along, looking out the window at it all.

As your pilot nears the airport, he will enter a standardized rectangular course called the *approach pattern*. With reduced power the engine will idle, the airplane will go into a *glide*. Don't be alarmed when the pilot turns to you and casually says, "We are on final approach." This does not mean all is lost. *Final approach* is just the standard term for the glide toward the runway that ends in the delicate curving out of the descent just over the runway and the gentle rolling of the wheels on this large turning ball in space called earth. You have returned.

If you still feel good about flying, here is what you can expect in terms of your student hours that lie ahead. For most people, at somewhere around ten hours of dual instructions, your pilot will casually step out of the airplane and ask you to take it around by yourself a couple of times. This unforgettable moment is your first *solo*.

There is a contradiction of terms here. As a brand-new solo student, a fledgling barely able to fly from the nest, you will quickly be set free on your student solo flight where technically you are pilot in command.

You will not really be a "pilot" yet. Though some students require more, the regulations require that you fly 35 to 40 hours minimum before you are qualified to fly with the examiner for your private pilot's check ride. Of this time, half will be more dual instruction and learning navigation, *cross-country* flying, a little bit of instrument flying and night flying. You will learn to use radio navigational aids, study aviation weather, and practice emergency procedures. By the time your instructor is ready to sign you off to the Federal Aviation Administration flight examiner, he will be as satisfied as you are that you are ready.

The private pilot's exam consists of two parts: a written exam and a flight test. Studying for the written test should be proceeding parallel to your increasing flying experience.

One of the best parts of learning to fly will be the early hands-on experience which begins in the first hour and the mystic first solo which seems to come on soon. It's a kind of a stunt, but not an uncommon one, that some airstruck kid, upon reaching his minimum qualifying age of 16 years, will go out on his birthday, start early and fly all day and solo on the same day.

Whether you are 16, 60, or older, there is no upper age limit to flying as long as you are fit enough to pass a rather basic medical examination. I know of two flight instructors who are both in their eighties and both still active, and I have at least one friend who passed his private pilot's exam and became eligible for Medicare the same day.

I know of several women who, having raised their families and stared without enthusiasm into a future of gin-and-tonics and bridge games, sallied forth to the airport to find out if grandmas can be taught to fly. Yes. And the experience would have to rank higher than being a halfway good Sunday painter in terms of discovering new beauty and a sense of satisfaction in your life.

It is a great asset among couples if the flying experience is at least shared at the language level if not in actual flying. One of the two is going to be coming home just bursting with enthusiasm and stories to tell for too long. One foot flying and one foot dragging can be a strain.

In my joyful travels as a speaker for aviation, one of the most common questions, nearly always asked from the audience when the wife is there, is this: "I love flying. It has become a rich and fulfilling part of my life, but now that I'm a private pilot and my wife could go with me, she won't. She says flying gives her a sick headache. Anything you can say to us?"

I always tell them the same thing. I say, "My first wife used to feel the same way about it."

><

In my enthusiasm here, don't let me give you a target-date fixation on "ten hours to solo, forty hours to private pilot exam." Those are only point-of-reference numbers. Students have soloed in as few as five hours, or more than fifteen. There are no fixed rules. When your instructor believes you can safely solo, he'll let you do it.

In those first hours of dual instruction the basics of flying will be easier done than they are told here in words. You can "fly"–that is, gently steer the plane where you want it to go–within the first hours or two.

From the beginning you will be taught to recognize a *stall* and how to cope with one. A stall begins when an airplane does not have enough airspeed for its flight conditions. One of my early instructors, Alfred Grant Vanneman, used to say, "I don't like stalls and the airplane doesn't either."

An ordinary, straight-ahead stall is recognized by the airplane slowing down, nose high, controls sluggish, a little shuddering as the wings lose their lift, and the loud honking of the stall warning horn in the cockpit. The cure for any stall is always the same: shove the yoke forward. Please don't ever forget that.

Practice stalls, done at altitude, are not hazardous, and learning to sense the approach of a stall is most valuable. Mastering the basics of stalls and recovery will not fill up an hour. The technique of landings and takeoffs will fill up nearly all your dual instruction time before solo.

You should be taxiing out and doing fairly decent takeoffs within the first hours of dual instruction. Exploring stalls will quickly remove the mask of the unknown from that fundamental part of flying safely, but landings just take us all longer to learn.

There are more variables to landing. They will require a more subtle touch and technique than you will have at first. Even some professional pilots are content with a sort of "ker-whump" arrival, but to me landings are still the most interesting part of flying, and although I was a slow learner (much to the exasperation of my mentors), I still see each new landing as a sort of challenge to feather it on better than I have ever done it before. I still get a lot of "ker-whumps," too.

Sometimes, tired at the end of a long day's journey, I'll thud my airplane in and as I open the throttle to go around and do it again I'm saying to myself, "Hell, I'm not going to let this fine trip end like that."

Chapter 20
One Wing in the Sunshine

During the 1960s and '70s, Lee "Pappy" Sheffield was the manager of Beaumont Municipal Airport. We called it the "grass airport." The place has since been lighted and paved, and Pappy has quietly retired, but he left his legends.

One was that the airport was open to all: to gliders, skydivers, model plane flyers, crop dusters, Sunday picnickers. The only person he ever ran off was a bearded youth who had an American flag sewn onto the seat of his jeans.

They say that if all the line boys Pappy gave part-time summer jobs and allowed to fly in his weary old Cessnas to rack up flying time, ever came back at once, the room would be full of airline captains, corporate pilots, and Air Force flyers.

Pappy would not lock up and go home if one of his chickens had not yet come home to roost. He would sit with a light in the window, waiting and listening. As flying grows more expensive and sophisticated, may there always be enough Pappys and grass airports.

But Pappy is best remembered for his advice about weather flying. He always said, "Keep one wing in the sunshine, and keep smiling." And if you asked him for a further explanation, he'd say, "You look at a pilot flying with at least one wing in the sunshine. He's relaxed and happy, he's leaning back enjoying himself, and he's smiling. But you look at that same pilot when he's flown into cloud. He's serious. He's leaning forward over the controls, frowning at the instruments, or trying to see out the windshield. He's not smiling anymore."

This was Pappy's way of telling his pilots that weather-related accidents account for the greatest number of air-crash fatalities. Why does this happen?

Does rain drown out airplane engines? No. Even the smallest aircraft engine can ingest an astonishing amount of rainwater and never miss a beat. The dual-ignition system of an airplane engine is so enshrouded and sheathed in metal that the ignition harness looks more like plumbing than wiring I've been in rainstorms so severe that it seemed as if I was flying up a fire hose.

The danger is not from the water; it is from reduced visibility.

><

Man is a visual-reference creature. As soon as he stands on solid ground, he knows which way is up and which way is down. His eyes must always have a visual reference to some horizon, somewhere.

Put him into something as shifty as an airplane, where the centrifugal forces in the top of a loop will make him feel as if he's sitting down when actually he's sitting "up," and he must look out the window and find the horizon line in order to "understand" his position.

Obscure the horizon line with cloud, rain, fog, and in less than two minutes, without instruments even the best pilot will not know which way is up ... until he spins out of the cloud base just before he hits the ground. That's why aircraft have all those artificial horizon instruments and turn-and-bank indicators—so they can be flown in weather when you can't see out the window.

Late in your student training, after you've gotten good enough to fly by reflex coordination and no longer need to concentrate on flying straight and level or making a gentle turn, you will be given a little *hood time* so that you can understand enough about flying on instruments (without visual reference) to get you down through a cloud layer, or make a 180-degree turn to fly back out of the clouds into the sunshine again.

The hood is a simple, light piece of headgear that looks sort of like a welder's helmet and limits your vision to the flight instruments. It's hinged at the temples, can be flipped up quickly if you need to see out, and is worn only with an instructor or observer beside you, unless you are cleared for instrument flying. Hood time will be a very interesting and valuable phase of your flight training, neither dangerous nor scary.

Flying with your hood on, the airplane will sound strangely subdued. Your senses are all focused down to your view of that small array of instruments on the panel. It's almost eerie, and you will be astonished at the conflicting messages that your body sends to your brain which must all be overridden by an intelligent interpretation of the instruments. The conflict comes from body sensors denied visual references. You can get part of the same effect by having someone twirl you in a swivel chair with your eyes closed, then trying to stand up. The staggering, falling sensation, and the illusion that you are still turning, ceases the instant you open your eyes.

The condition is called spatial disorientation, and it's caused by the balance sensors of your inner ear, which must function in association with visual references. The human balance system, located in the inner ear, consists of three semi-circular canals, each partially filled with fluid and each reporting on a different axis of movement. This information is sensed by the brain from hair-like nerve endings within the semi-circular canals. When you abruptly stop turning, the fluid sloshes on a ways, giving a false turning sensation to the brain, which the eye cancels out by telling the brain that you are not really turning.

><

Flying when you can't see out the window, and being in a plane which can turn freely about all three axes itself, can create some powerful wrong sensations. The only thing you can do to correct for this is to concentrate on those little artificial horizons and turn instruments.

The results can sometimes be comic.

It's not uncommon for a pilot to "get the leans." His training and logic tell him that he is flying straight and level as indicated on the instruments. But his deep body muscles are so sure that the plane is banking one way or the other that he may end up flying level, yet leaned way over to one side in the cockpit. In serious two-pilot instrument flying, that's when one says to the other, "I've gone vertigo and you got it."

Most experienced instrument pilots avoid a lot of excessive head movement when concentrating on instrument flying. Bending down to pick up a chart off the floor is one of the worst things you can do. The sensation upon straightening up may be that the plane has just snap-rolled to the left, and the pilot may actually snap-roll to the right to "save" it.

Back in the open-cockpit biplane days, when a pilot was caught on top of a layer of clouds, rather than try to descend through it and get into an inadvertent and unknown-direction spin, he would just pull up, stall it, and spin down through the cloud layer on purpose. The old planes descended at 500 feet per minute in a spin, the pilot knew which way the spin had begun, and you might say that in a sort of wild brave way he was making a controller descend–hoping all the while for just a quick glimpse of the horizon as he fell out the belly of a cloud.

It is far better to put in a little hood time. But this in no way qualifies you as an instrument-rated pilot. To be able to take off, navigate cross-country, and use the instrument systems to land, is a separate art and skill. It is one that I heartily recommend you learn as soon as you are qualified with 200 hours of pilot flight time.

Learning to fly on instruments will take about as many instructional hours as it did just to change yourself from a groundling. To keep his instrument ticket current, an instrument pilot must have six hours of flight experience within the preceding six months. Within those six hours, he must also have flown at least six instrument approaches–for that's the dicey part of it, following those needles right on down to near the ground. If an instrument pilot has let his rating lapse (rust would be a better word for it), then he can get re-qualified by flying with an instructor.

I do urge that you set a goal of becoming an instrument-rated pilot as soon as you can. Without it, your airplane might as well be a submarine when the clouds hang low. You can't go. With an instrument rating, you will understand and utilize all the equipment in your airplane and the magnificent system of charted airways, their ads, beacons, and ground controllers. You will think, speak, and fly more like a professional pilot and fit better into such traffic.

Your instrument rating will be the line of demarcation between being a good ole boy pasture pilot, and being a pro.

Until you become a proficient instrument pilot, the best and most valuable maneuver you can learn is the 180-degree turn. A 180-degree turn simply turns you around and heads you back the way you came. The maneuver itself is so simple that you will know how to do it after your first hour of dual instruction. But knowing when to do a 180-degree turn, and drumming into your consciousness the notion that you will do a 180-degree turn if the weather looks doubtful, is something you may have to work on as long as you fly. For those who don't learn this, the National Transportation Safety Board accident reports read monotonously the same: "VFR pilot continued flight into IFR weather conditions." Then they tell how many fatalities there were.

The pattern of these weather-related wrecks, which are probably your greatest hazard in private flying, varies so little that such accidents have earned a popular nickname in aviation: they are called "graveyard spirals."

Here is how it's done:

The non-instrument-rated pilot enters into cloud, fog, snow, or whatever it takes to obscure the horizon line. Within about ninety seconds, he is getting false turning sensations from his inner ear. Unable to interpret his flight instruments, which are beginning to twirl before his eyes, and the mounting confusion and panic, he wrestles the perfectly good-flying airplane into a turn. In the turn, possibly in an unknown direction, the nose drops and speed builds up. The pilot, hearing the rising sounds of speed, interprets this correctly as dangerous, but his instinctive control movements are wrong.

He knows he's diving; he may even be able to see the altimeter unwinding, so he pulls back on the yoke to pull up out of the dive. In a steep turn this only tightens the turn, gives him a seat-of-the-pants G-load message that he may be pulling up, but since he's already in a steep turn, the up-elevator only tightens the turn and the diving spiral worsens. The pilot now realizes that nothing is working and the plane has gotten away from him.

It is a terrifying experience. If the airplane does not exceed its redline maximum speed and break up in flight, it augers into the ground from this graveyard spiral.

><

During my radio days, I worked with J.P. Richardson, the night announcer who was writing songs and hoping to make it big as the "Big Bopper."

J.P., or Jape as we called him, reported a weather-related light-plane crash on the ten-o'clock news. Knowing I was a pilot, he asked me why light planes fell out of the sky in bad weather. It's nearly impossible to explain or visualize the experience of spatial disorientation and the graveyard spiral, so I invited him to come fly with me the next day so I could show him.

In clear weather, flying one of Pappy's old Cessna 150s, I asked Jape to shut his eyes and describe to me what he felt the airplane was doing. I simulated an out-of-control spiral, which was safe enough while I could see the horizon.

Jape said "We are turning. Now we are diving. Now you are pulling up out of the dive. No ... no ... I dunno."

He had just rehearsed his death, which came just a few months later, after his "Chantilly Lace" became a million-seller, and while he was on tour with Buddy Holly and Richie Valens.

They had finished a rock and roll concert in Iowa and had chartered a Bonanza to get to the next town, next show.

The charter pilot had failed his instrument flight exam but considered himself good enough on instruments to take off in the middle of the night in a snowstorm. The wreck was found about two minutes from the field where they took off. The plane had spiraled straight in.

"The Day the Music Died" is the way their death is remembered in song.

But I will always be haunted, wondering how much Jape knew and what he was thinking in those last few seconds.

><

I still could not believe that a pilot could lose control of a plane just from flying through clouds.

My own "born again" experience happened on a brave Texas to New York flight when I had precious few hours in my log book. I was homeward bound in a little straight-backed Cessna 150, running beneath an overcast, between rows of mountains, down in the Shenandoah Valley. I knew this was risky, but I had gotten away with flying under low ceilings before.

What I was not paying attention to was the *dew point-temperature spread*. This vital information is broadcast by the Flight Service Station along with altimeter settings and wind direction. When the dew point and the temperature become the same, fog forms, as it did in my beautiful valley whose rocks and hills are so celebrated in song and verse.

I crept lower, until windmills were flashing by, and farmers on tractors were ducking and shaking their fists.

There is just no place in this scenic rocky part of the country to force-land an airplane. I considered a controlled crash, stalling in, flaps down. One could survive an excursion through thickets and fields like that, but it would total the airplane. This is when I found out about the silly instinct pilots have against deliberately wrecking a good-running airplane.

The fog thickened. I could only see down through the corner of the windshield for about fifty yards ahead. But glimmers of sunlight told me that the overcast was thin. As you are doing now, I had read all the horror stories of what happens if you fly into clouds, but I decided it probably didn't apply to me. Anyone could set up a 500-foot-a-minute standard rate of climb; just sit still, and in two minutes the little Cessna should pop out on top in sunshine like a mullet from a gray pond.

With the cold, deliberate detachment that a suicide must feel as he loads the clip, I set up the climb and entered into the clouds. Why not? I was lost already, mountains on both sides, and when you're scud-running you are usually too low to pick up any VOR navigational beacons to find out where you are. The losing streak quickly compounds itself, like a burnt-out crap shooter at the tables in Vegas.

So I bet my heap.

Actually, it wasn't so bad. It was cool and quiet in the muted cloud–sort of like flying inside a ping pong ball. I didn't move or touch anything. And sure enough, a bright silvery light soon flooded the cockpit. I was almost out of the top. I glanced up to see how soon.

Moved my head. That did it. Vertigo.

The little Cessna fell into a spin. I had no idea of which way, but they taught spin training in those days, and I urge that you ask your instructor to teach spins to you now, even though this sickening sort of violent maneuver is no longer required in private pilot's training. From my past instruction, I recognized the sound of a spin. I knew I would be dead in less than sixty seconds. Again, the feeling was one of detachment, tinged with regret.

My mind was flashing up all the spin-related events it knew. An instructor's voice came back to me: "The folks in Wichita didn't really want this little airplane to spin easily. That's why if you just cut power, turn it loose; it stops spinning all by itself and goes into a gentle sliding turn."

><

That was the straw that floated to me, as I was drowning in this whirlpool.

I pulled back the throttle, took my feet off the rudders, folded my arms across my chest, and gazed sort of forlornly down out the corner of the windshield, wondering if this would hurt much.

I heard the plane quiet down, slow down, but I still had no idea of what it was doing. Then the green blur of earth, and at the same instant we glided out from under the cloud bottom at about 200 feet in an almost wings-level gentle turn. I was alive.

More hair-raising scud running led to a pool of sunlight in the next valley. I got into a pond of light and tried to spiral upward. This is when I learned that a light airplane already straining to stay at altitude during a steeply banked turn just doesn't have enough lift or thrust left in it to climb. I sank to the bottom of my well of light like a gasping, dying fish.

Over the next hill, and flashing by one more silo, there was a long trough of sunlight. It was long enough and wide enough for me to climb in it, wings level, make a steep turn as the wall of cloud approached, then level out and climb like mad again, a pattern similar to an escalator and its level turnaround landings at each floor.

I broke out on top, found distant Atlanta on the VOR, and went forth a free man, to sin to more.

Atlanta was in the clear, but I found that I could not remember the two-digit runway number I was cleared to land on, nor translate this information into the required logic of identifying that runway by its compass heading. I flew well, landed well, but seemed to be in a robot-like trance. Atlanta was not as crowded with jet traffic in those days, and the tower gave up on me and said just land on the runway I was pointed at, since I seemed to be landing on it anyway.

><

Later, I discussed this incapacity to reason or think with a friend who is a neurosurgeon. He listened to the entire tale, and said I was in a state of delayed shock. It's an extreme condition, just before the screaming state, when a person is confronted with his own certain death. He said the thinking part of my brain had already shut down, and the more primitive motor controls of the old brain were flying the plane well enough.

The horror went on after landing. At a motel, taking a hot bath, I began to think the bath was red with blood and that I was actually back in the Shenandoah Valley, a part of the shredded aluminum hanging from broken, fog-dripping trees. I fled the bath in terror, dressed, and went into the crowded snack bar.

There was one empty stool. I slipped onto it, and neither person on either side made a move. I sat there, and the waitress–busy back and forth behind the counter, friendly, smiling to the others–never even glanced at me.

The horrors began to come back: the spin, that fog-filled valley, me dead in the wreck. Was I only dreaming that I had escaped because I wanted to live so much? Was I sitting here in this café, or in some supernatural nether world?

Then that plump blond Georgia girl finally looked straight at me and said, "May I help you, suh?" She is probably still wondering why the gaunt man with the strange, hollow eyes first offered to marry her, then asked for a cup of black coffee, "and another one every time you see me."

Chapter 21
It Only Hurts When
I flap My Arms

My last flight couldn't have been as perfect had it been scripted as romantic fiction. It was home from Houston on a clear night alone in my own plane. A passage of places as familiar as the feel of a loved one's face.

I had spent the long day at Houston, frying out on the ramp at Hobby Airport, doing videotape interviews of teams of pilots who had been invited to come fly a new three-engine, six-million-dollar French bizjet.

The interviews were being conducted on a ramp teeming with expensive hardware—Lears, Citations, Falcons and other exotica wheezing by. So many little expensive hard rubber tires nibbling at the cement that all the ordinary old fat-wheeled flying machines like mine had been shunted out of the way and left out in the high grass, like extra cardboard boxes.

All day as I interviewed keen-eyed, carefully spoken corporate pilots, I was looking over their shoulders at my own airplane sitting out there, all sun-faded and oil-streaked and daydreaming about her. She is a disgraceful-looking airplane compared to all the bright jewelry around us, but unlike these other creatures, she belongs to a single person. To me.

You ever notice how an old Mooney sitting out in the grass always looks like her socks are down around her ankles? If you opened the door of my Mooney's cabin, it would smell like old tennis shoes stored in a filling station, but there is a document inside a yellowed plastic frame on the bulkhead that says I am the sole owner of this frazzled little beast. They got a piece of paper like that on the bulkhead of every one of those jets, but you don't find any of those pilots' names on them.

We edited film until midnight. It was a really sharp crew with some space-age computer-edit, split-frame stuff, but even with all those whiz consoles going for us, my eyeballs were flat as fried eggs by midnight. I got to thinking about all those accident reports where the Feds peel back the layers and find out how fatigued the pilot was, and I decided to play it cool and hang it up for the night in Houston.

I spent 90 minutes trying to acquire a cheese-burger and a cab across town, and still hadn't made it but was zingy enough mad to know that in 40 minutes I could be home, could get there in my own plane and not have to wake up still in Houston.

>＜

Part of the decision to go fly myself was the moonlight and stars; I could see all the way to El Paso.

The old Mooney was glistening with dew as I felt around in the wet cabin and brought her little starry panel to life. She was fresh and feisty from her annual at the healing hands of Charlie Dugosh, who happens to be the world's best Mooney mechanic.

Now, in the center of the night, the whip-crack urgency of daytime Houston radio traffic had snoozed off to the secret compacts of those who keep the night watch.

"You don't bother me, I won't bother you."

Two-Seven November became a set of winking lights curving away, monitored only from the dark windows of the tower that watches over HOU.

The little airplane settled down at once. You ever notice how old engines seem to run fatter at night? And there were none of the daytime pranks of an airplane that sometimes wants to skew along sideways.

My backbone and my old airplane's spine lay in perfect alignment in the purple night.

The white-shafted San Jacinto battleground monument and other favorite sights drifted into view. I thought of Sam Houston's army camped down there, where Interstate 10 now carries a bright berry row of auto lights, and where more Texans and Mexicans kill each other with their cars every year than did all those armies combined. That's a part of the smugness of flying your own plane over the Interstate.

The heading to home cuts across Old River, lost and old, and the Trinity River bottom lands where pirate ghosts lie in the permanent fog wisps. Some of the first stories I sold to *Flying* were about sneaking through there in Cessnas.

The flight path quarters across the terraced rice fields where the broad-wing Stearman biplanes will bank their greetings to the morning sun. I have come this far flying a 450 two-holer.

I've looked at the world from every conceivable angle from between those taut wings, and I've shouted in the slipstream for the joy of it.

I don't think I was ever more alive than those summers when I groaned around in those old biplanes.

Then it was time to start letting down for Pappy's grass airport. Go on, drop the nose and don't throttle back; let her sizzle some, but don't play with it out over that black-hole north approach. Gear down, green light, really an instrument approach, though no longer as hair-raising as it used to be before we got lights and pavement. We used to sink into the dark grass and wonder where they left the tractor.

The landing was a kisser. A no-brakes rollout and swing around by my old tin stall. I sat there a minute with all the switches off and listened to the dying whine of the gyros. What a rich feeling of accomplishment. I breasted the cowling, spinner nuzzled under my arm, and rolled her in, then spent my shameless magic moment with this molded warm-smelling airplane. I said to her, "Thank you, Mooney, for bringing me home again. You're a good airplane." Then I walked to a pay phone for the swagger call to Diane. "Hi babe, once again I have cheated fate." Our private thing. We both know air-planes are not like that.

A few days later I was slated to fly solo to Memphis for an interview. I had the seizure that mid-night, in my sleep. Woke up a day or so later in the hospital.

The prognosis is good, all but the pilot's license.

But you know what's funny? I still carry it. I cherish the 21 years I was a licensed pilot. The richest years of my life. I only owned 27 November a year and a half.

Acknowledgments

Rebecca Kinnard, my Aunt Becky, is a source of love and strength for me. Until she passed away in 2014, my mom relied for advice and support on Aunt Becky. For me, after losing both parents, and having a disability, Aunt Becky is a source of strength. She decorates my life with joy and love, as she does for her family and many others. My well-being centers on this remarkable woman. It is my good luck to be her niece.

Rosie Walker and my mom became friends when they were in the eighth grade. Rosie has held my hand through the process of completing this book, a project that she and my mom started working on a dozen years ago. I thank Rosie for helping me to realize the vision my mom had for my life.

Jenny T. Baxter
December 2021

Printed in Great Britain
by Amazon